SPAN

Learn the Basics

By Franco Sanz

© 2013

All Rights Reserved. No part of this publication may be reproduced in any form or by any means, including scanning, photocopying, or otherwise without prior written permission of the copyright holder.

Disclaimer and Terms of Use: The Author and Publisher has strived to be as accurate and complete as possible in the creation of this book, notwithstanding the fact that he does not warrant or represent at any time that the contents within are accurate due to the rapidly changing nature of the Internet. While all attempts have been made to verify information provided in this publication, the Author and Publisher assumes no responsibility for errors, omissions, or contrary interpretation of the subject matter herein. Any perceived slights of specific persons, peoples, or organizations are unintentional. In practical advice books, like anything else in life, there are no guarantees of income made. This book is not intended for use as a source of legal, business, accounting or financial advice. All readers are advised to seek services of competent professionals in legal, business, accounting, and finance field.

First Printing, 2012

Printed in the United States of America

NOTE: Some of you may experience difficulties with the pronunciation of the Spanish vowels, consonants and syllables. To help you in this process, we suggest going to **www.forvo.com**. This interactive site will assist you in learning to pronounce words correctly.

One Spanish or Many?

Hello, welcome to a new experience of learning Spanish. The goal of this book is to give you the initial step to help you become proficient in the use of the Spanish language, whether you want to use it in your travels, for business, or to engage in conversations with relatives and friends whose mother tongue is Spanish.

The first thing that needs to be pointed out is that there is more than one Spanish language. This statement may baffle you, but think about English for one minute. The differences you will find between the English spoken in Perth, Australia, the English spoken in South Africa, and the one spoken in Boston, are similar to the Spanish spoken in Madrid and the Spanish they speak in Santiago de Chile.

So I want to encourage you not to feel afraid of these differences because you can make yourself understood. For every slang word in Spanish, there is another plain word that expresses the same meaning; you just have to ask for it!

In this book, we will focus on the Spanish spoken in South America. You will also find notes dedicated to studying the differences with the Spanish from Spain. After you finish reading this book, you will be ready to communicate effectively in Spanish in everyday situations, ask for directions, ask questions, and find out about the people around you.

The content of the book is structured and designed to give you examples of real conversations with clear grammar explanations so you know exactly what to say and why to use each word. Common expressions and vocabulary complete this course so you will have all the basic elements to communicate effectively in Spanish. However, your dedication to the lessons included in this book is essential for your success.

We strongly recommend that you find additional sources of contact with the Spanish language, such as newspapers that offer a Spanish version, magazines, and even entertainment news! One trick we would like to mention is to find something you are passionate about –it can be sports, music, movies, fashion, furniture, cooking, cars, etc. Read brief articles about your topic of choice in Spanish, especially after finishing this book.

You will see that all you need to do to master the language is to actually get as much practice as possible.

It is time to start this journey, so get ready to enjoy!

Table of Contents

The Alphabet

Pronunciation

   Focus on: Pronunciation

Classification of Words

   Sustantivos – Nouns

   Adjetivos – Adjectives

   Articulos – Articles

   Verbos – Verbs

   Preposiciones – Prepositions

   Conectores – Connectors

Greetings and Introductory words

Verb To Be I: Ser

Noun Gender

Subject Pronouns

   All About Adjectives

Possessive Adjectives

Comparisons

Affirmative, Negative, and Interrogative Sentences

The Present Tense

   Verb To Be II: Estar

Present Progressive Tense

Past Simple Tense

The Future Tense

Appendix

   Spanish Regular Verbs

   Measurement Conversion

Are You Interested In Learning More Spanish?

Final Words

The Alphabet

The Spanish alphabet, or abecedario, is made up of 27 letters, according to the latest edition of the Real Academia **Española**, the reference that sets grammar and vocabulary rules that govern the Spanish language. Here are the letters and their names. Later on you will find examples of how to pronounce each letter. Keep in mind that each letter in Spanish has a sharp, clear sound, and only **one sound**.

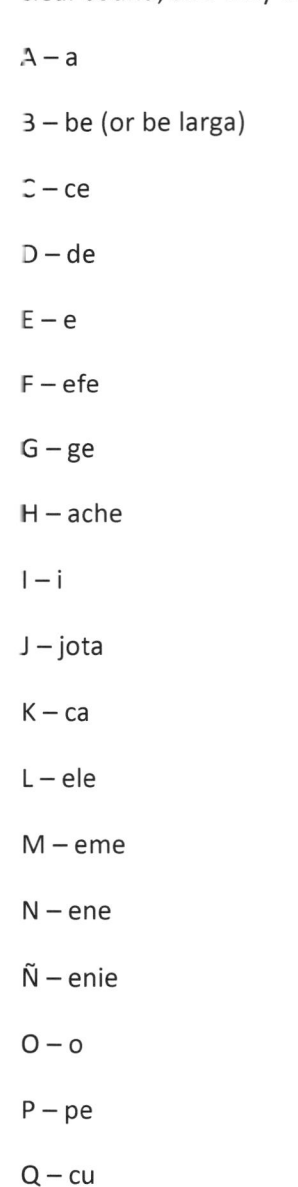

A – a

B – be (or be larga)

C – ce

D – de

E – e

F – efe

G – ge

H – ache

I – i

J – jota

K – ca

L – ele

M – eme

N – ene

Ñ – enie

O – o

P – pe

Q – cu

R – ere

S - ese

T – te

U – u

V – ve / uve (Spain) / ve corta (Latin America)

W – doble ve / uve doble (Spain)

X – equis

Y – i griega

Z - zeta

Notice that some letters take different names whether you are in Spain or Latin America. While the same rules of spelling apply to both regions, the names may change. For example, someone in Spain will say that this letter, "V" is called Uve, while someone in Mexico will say its name is Ve or Ve Corta, as opposed to Be Larga.

Pronunciation

To help you understand pronunciation, you will find next a list of the letters and the sound they produce. Like we said before, the sounds, especially those of the vowels, are sharp and clear. Many of the consonants, however, have a similar pronunciation as in English, which will make them easier to learn!

A – Like in **a**pple, **fa**ther

B – Like in **b**oot, **b**ad

C – Before **e** and **i**, it sounds like **c** in **c**entury; before **a**, **o** and **u**, it sounds like **c** in **c**ourt

Ch – This is a combination of the two letters, although in the past it was considered a letter on its own. It sounds like **ch** in **ch**eck

D – Like **d** in **d**airy

E – Like e in p**e**n

F – Like f in **f**lour

G – Before **e** and **i**, it sounds like a strong **j**, or like **h** in **h**igh. Before **a**, **o** and **u**, it sounds like **g** in **g**uide. In combinations like **gue** and **gui**, it sounds like **gue**st or **gui**lty

H – This is a **silent** letter. In foreign words, like **H**awaii or **h**ámster, it takes the English pronunciation and it sounds like **j**.

I – Like **e** in d**ee**p

J – Mostly like **h** in **h**ip

K – Like **c** in **c**ucumber, or **k** in **k**id. However this letter is not often used in Spanish, mostly in foreign words.

L – Like **l** in **l**aughter

M – Like **m** in **m**an

N – Like **n** in **n**ow

Ñ – Like n+y+vowel. For example, **ñu** sounds similar to **new**

O – Like **o** in f**o**r

P – Like **p** in **p**ink

Q – Like **q** in **q**uestion. This letter is always followed by a u, but in combinations **que** and **qui**, the u is silent, and the sound is like the English **k**.

R – This letter has a "soft" and "hard" sound depending on its position in the word and the letter that it precedes. At the beginning of a word, the sound is strong, think of "grrr;" it is also strong after **l**, **n** or **s** in the middle of a word (like in so**n**risa, a**l**rededor). Also in the middle of a word, the r may appear doubled: a**rr**iero, e**rr**or. In these cases, the sound is strong like "grrr." The "soft" r sound appears in the middle of a word where there is a single r, and it is not preceded by l, n or s: aroma, valorar. The soft sound of **r** can be compared to the **r** in serve.

S – Like **s** in **s**ick

T – While it does not have an exact equivalent in English, it is similar to **t** in **t**ongue and **t**ea.

U – Like a short **oo** in b**oo**m. When combined with another vowel, it sounds like **w** in t**w**ist. Finally, in the case of **gue** and **gui,** it is silent.

V – Like **v** in **v**alue. Often it is also similar to the Spanish letter **b**, as most speakers don't make an identifiable different sound for b and v.

W – Used only in foreign words and the pronunciation varies. In general, speakers use either v or b, like in voice, or hui, like in winner.

X – Like ks, similar to exit

Y – Sounds like the Spanish vowel **i** when it is used as a word to mean "and" (example: Sam y Sonia, Sam and Sonia) and at the end of certain words, like soy (sounds like soi). Before another vowel, it sounds like **j** in **j**ust.

Z – Like a soft **c**, or like a **th** in **th**ief

Focus on: Pronunciation

To learn to speak a language, any language, there are no shortcuts. The secret is to overcome your inhibitions and practice as much as possible. You may want to postpone talking to a native Spanish speaker, if you have the chance to do so, but in reality, the earlier you start practicing in a real world situation, the better. This book will provide you with lots of phrases that you can actually use in the real world, but they will be no good unless you practice what you are learning. To get started, mark this part of the book as important. Separate the *abecedario* into vowels and consonants:

a – e- i – o – u

b – c – d – f – g – h – j – k – l – m – n – ñ – p – q – r – s – t – v – w – x – y – z

Now repeat them using the cues above to reproduce the sounds in Spanish. Remember, one letter, one sound. If you have a bilingual dictionary, look up simple words starting with each letter and try to say it out loud. Tip: the dictionary usually includes the phonetic pronunciation for each word. If you still do not own a bilingual dictionary, I strongly suggest that you get one.

Classification of Words

Throughout this book, you will find a number of grammar concepts that may or may not sound familiar to you. To make sure you understand every single aspect presented in this elementary Spanish course, we are including a brief description of some of the concepts used. Let's start with a classification of words. Why is this important? While grammar is not the goal, you must understand the kind of word that is expected to appear in any given sentence, why it takes that place, and why you may not use a different class of word, for example, when this changes the meaning of a sentence. You do not need to memorize these definitions, just come back to them whenever you are in doubt; it will surely come in handy. So let's dive right in.

Sustantivos – Nouns

Nouns or sustantivos in Spanish, designate objects and subjects. A flower, a house, a child, they are all nouns. We can divide nouns into two categories: common and proper. Common nouns are also divided into concrete (animals, people and objects), and abstract (feelings, quality, ideas, etc). Proper nouns are proper names of cities and people (for example, New York, Madrid, Rubén, Carlos, etc.)

Adjetivos – Adjectives

Adjectives are words that we use to describe things, people, and animals. In other words, we use them to describe nouns. Some adjectives describe color, shape, and other qualities. Examples of adjectives are: small, yellow, square, short, and young. In general, it can be said that in the Spanish language, adjectives come after nouns, although this is not necessarily a rule, since we can sometimes find adjectives before nouns for reasons of emphasis or style.

Articulos – Articles

Articles are words that precede a noun and they can be divided into two categories: definite and indefinite. The word "the" is a definite article because it "defines" the noun it refers to, whereas "a" or "an" are indefinite articles because it does not specify exactly which noun it refers to.

Verbos – Verbs

Verbs or verbos in Spanish, are words that convey an action, a state, or an occurrence. Common verbs are: put, do, learn, say, talk, among others. In Spanish, verbs take a different ending depending not only on the tense they are in, but also depending on the subject doing the action. You will learn to conjugate verbs later in this book.

Preposiciones – Prepositions

Prepositions are words that describe relations or functions. It is really easy to identify them in English: for, from, to, in, on, over, until, among others. You will use these in Spanish in numerous sentences and phrases, as they are as common in English as they are in Spanish.

Conectores – Connectors

As the name indicates, they describe a connection between two parts in a sentence. Some connectors in English are: and, but, nevertheless, or, however, among others.

Greetings and Introductory words

Dialogue 1 – Four students meet at a business workshop.

Elena: Hola, mi nombre es Elena. ¿Cómo te llamas? = *Hello, my name is Elena, What's your name?*

Lucas: Hola Elena. Soy Lucas. Y él es Rodrigo. = *Hello Elena. I'm Lucas. And he is Rodrigo.*

Rodrigo: Hola, ¿cómo estás? = *Hi, how are you?*

Elena: Bien, ¿y tú? = *I'm good. How are you?*

Rodrigo: Muy bien, gracias. = *I'm great, thank you.*

Ana: Buenos días. Soy Ana. ¿Y ustedes? = *Good morning. I'm Ana, and you are?*

Lucas: Buenos días Ana, soy Lucas. Ella se llama Elena, y él es Rodrigo. = *Good morning Ana, I'm Lucas. Her name is Elena, and he is Rodrigo.*

Elena: ¿De dónde eres, Ana? = *Ana, where are you from?*

Ana: Soy de California, ¿y ustedes? = *I'm from California, how about you?*

Rodrigo: Yo soy de España. ¿De dónde eres tú, Elena? = *I'm from Spain. Where are you from, Elena?*

Elena: Yo soy de Argentina. = *I am from Argentina*

Lucas: Yo vengo de Colombia. = *I come from Colombia*

Rodrigo: Elena, luces muy joven, ¿cuántos años tienes? = *Elena, you look very young, how old are you?*

Elena: ¡Gracias! Tengo 28 años. ¿Y ustedes? = *Thank you! I'm 28 years old, how about you?*

Ana: Yo tengo 31 años. = *I'm 31 years old*

Rodrigo: Yo tengo 29 años, y lucas tiene 25 años. = *I'm 29 and Lucas is 25.*

Ana: La clase está por comenzar... = *The class is about to start...*

Meeting new people

When visiting in a Spanish speaking country, it is a sign of good manners to greet people in Spanish. While this is not mandatory, it shows the Spanish speakers around you that you respect them and you are "making an effort" to make yourself understood in their language. Even if you are not yet ready to commit to a whole conversation in Spanish, a greeting can make a difference and set the tone for the rest of the interaction. People usually appreciate it when tourists and visitors can speak at least a few words in their native language, and may instantly consider you *simpático* or *cordial* – nice or kind, in English.

Others ways of greeting people

When meeting somebody:

¿Que tal? – *informal = What's up?*

¿Como estás? – *informal = How are you?*

¿Como está usted? – *formal = How do you do?*

¿Como le va? – *rather informal = How are you doing?*

Mucho gusto – *formal = Nice to meet you*

Encantado (de conocerlo) – *rather formal = It's a pleasure to meet you*

General greetings

Buenos días – *formal / neutral = Good morning*

Buenas Tardes – *formal / neutral = Good afternoon*

Buenas noches – *formal / neutral = Good evening*

Adiós – *formal = Goodbye*

Chau – *informal = Bye*

Hasta luego – *informal = See you later*

Hasta pronto – *informal = See you soon*

Que tenga usted un buen día – *formal = Have a nice day*

Verb To Be I: Ser

The verb "to be" has two meanings in Spanish, or to be more exact, two different uses. For this reason, most students of Spanish as a second language often confuse the two. Think of this expression: "In Spanish, there is more than one way to be." Let's start by taking a look at the verb SER. In the dialogue, the speakers use the verb ser in the following sentences:

Soy Ana = I'm Ana

Soy Lucas = I'm Lucas

Soy de España = I'm from Spain

They are talking about an essence, characteristics that will not change, because they are permanent. We can say that the verb SER in Spanish is used for talking about the essence of someone or something. Now the Spanish language is famous for its conjugation system, so let's revise now how to conjugate the verb Ser for all other subjects.

Yo soy = I am

Tú eres = You are

Él es = He is

Ella es = She is

Nosotros somos = We are

Ustedes son = You (plurar) are

Ellos son = They are

How can you use the verb Ser in Spanish sentences? You can use this verb to state a variety of essential characteristics, take a look at these sentences from Lucas and Ana:

Ana: Soy Ana. Soy vendedora. Soy de California. Soy muy sociable. / Ana: I'm Ana. I'm a saleswoman. I'm from California. I'm very outgoing.

Lucas: Soy Lucas. Soy abogado. Soy de Colombia. Soy inteligente y amable. / Lucas: I'm Lucas. I'm a lawyer. I'm from Colombia. I'm smart and kind.

Some of the characteristics that you can describe using the verb Ser are:

Nationality – Occupation – Personality – Appearance – Time of the day – Political/religious belief – Relations.

We'll get back to some of these later. Now, let's take a look at how to form negative and interrogative sentences using the verb Ser. Read the following conversation:

Elena: Ana, ¿tú eres periodista? = Elena: Ana, are you a journalist?

Ana: No, no lo soy. Soy vendedora. = Ana: No, I'm not. I'm a saleswoman.

Elena: Ah, y tú, Lucas, ¿eres vendedor también? = Elena: Oh, and you Lucas, are you a salesman, too?

Lucas: No, no lo soy. Soy abogado. = Lucas: No, I'm not. I'm a lawyer.

Rodrigo: Elena, ¿tú eres de Grecia? = Rodrigo: Elena, are you from Greece?

Elena: No, soy de Argentina. = Elena: No, I'm from Argentina.

In Spanish, the order of words in interrogative sentences is not strict. In fact, there are a number of ways to form a question. For this reason, intonation is really important to make it clear that you are in fact asking about something. One of the most widely forms of making questions is placing the verb Ser before the "essential quality" you are referring to, such as this:

¿Eres abogado? = Are you a lawyer?

¿Tú eres sociable? = Are you outgoing?

¿Eres vendedora? = Are you a saleswoman?

To form negative sentences, you simply need to add the word "no" before the verb ser, which makes it really easy to understand. The verb Ser will need to be conjugated. Here are some examples:

No soy abogado = I'm not a lawyer

No soy de Grecia = I'm not from Greece

No eres vendedor = You are not a salesman

No eres Lucas = You are not Lucas

Noun Gender

As strange as it may sound, in Spanish, every noun has a gender, in other words, you will have to think in terms of he/she when you talk about nouns. Now that may be a little hard to do at first, but there are some simple rules that you can use to get accustomed to thinking in terms of gender. For example, would you say that a car is male or female? What about a towel? Tricky, right? Here are some examples:

El televisor = The TV

La heladera = The fridge

El cuaderno = The notebook

La bicicleta = The bicycle

As a general rule, we will say that when a noun ends in –o or –e, it is masculine and when a noun ends in –a, it's feminine. This rule becomes important when you realize that most singular common nouns end in either –a, -e or –o.

Now, it is often said that Spanish speakers tend to overuse articles before a noun. Articles are those little words that precede a noun. For example, in English the words: the, a, an, are articles. Let's talk a little more about articles and how to use them according to noun gender.

Think about the difference between *"a"* and *"the"*. When you say, "I want a yellow skirt", you are probably at a clothing store, asking to see *any* yellow skirt they may have. You are likely undecided about which one to buy, so the skirt is not defined. For this reason you use an indefinite article: a (or an). Once you have seen all the skirts they have, you will probably decide to buy one: you can define which skirt you liked the best, so you say, "I want the short skirt". In this case, "the" is used to define which skirt you want. It is called a definite article, because it defines, among a number of options, which one you are referring to.

In Spanish, these articles are represented by *el/la*, which mean *the*, and *un/una*, which mean *a* or *an*. How do these words relate to nouns?

Remember that we said you need to think of the gender of a noun? Well, depending on the gender, you will have to choose el or la, and un or una.

Here are some examples:

El auto = The car

Un auto = A car

La casa = The house

Una casa = A house

El perfume = The fragrance

Un perfume = A fragrance

La cartera = The purse

Una cartera = A purse

See how these combine? When a noun ends in –a, you will need to use la or una, depending on whether you are talking about a particular item, or any item within a group.

If the noun ends in –e or –o, you will need to use el or un, using the same logic.

Un/el oso = a/the bear

Un/el disco = a/the record

Un/el tomate = a/the tomato

Una/la palabra = a/the word

Una/la remera = a/the t-shirt

Una/la torta = a/the cake

Exceptions
Of course, there are exceptions to this rule. Some nouns end in a different letter, making it harder to remember which article to use. But this list will

surely help you identify them easily and assign them the correct article, el or la, un or una:

Nouns ending in –tud, -dad and -tad are feminine. They take la and una. Take a look:

La liber**tad** = Freedom

Una vir**tud** = Virtue

La felici**dad** = Happiness

Nouns ending in –ión are feminine. This includes nouns ending in –ción, -sión, -gión

La prisión = Prison

La región = Region

Una pasión = Passion

Another case is nouns ending in –umbre. They also take a feminine article:

La incertidumbre = The uncertainty

La cumbre = The peak

La legumbre = The legume

Nouns ending in –triz are feminine. There are not too many, but here are some examples:

La institutriz = The governess

Una cicatriz = The scar

La matriz = The matrix

Many abstract nouns end in –ez. They are considered feminine, and you should use la/una:

La testarudez = Stubbornness

Una exquisitez = Exquisiteness

La inmadurez = Immaturity

So far it looks like there are more exceptions than the actual rules. But you will become accustomed once you start seeing and reading texts in Spanish. Let's revise the noun endings that take a feminine form:

–tud, -dad, -tad, –ción, -sión, -gión, -íon, –umbre, -triz, -ez

When you see a noun with these endings, you will want to pay attention and remember that they are feminine.

Now, remember that nouns ending in –e and –o are masculine. There are some exceptions to this rule too, but only in a limited number of words. Here are the ones you need to memorize:

El planeta = The planet

El sofá = The sofa

El día = The day

El mapa = The map

It won´t take you too much time to memorize these, as they are only four. El día is a set of words that you will use a lot, so is el sofá, and el mapa, especially if you are fond of travelling.

Now take a look at these words:

El plasma = The plasma

El fantasma = The ghost

El tema = The theme

Some noun ending in –ma are masculine, especially those of Greek origins. Why should you pay attention to this? Because we said that nouns ending in –a are feminine, and this is an exception to that rule.

Nouns ending in –ista, -crata, -ente, and –ante can be used for both feminine and masculine nouns. Here are some examples of words with the above mentioned endings, and how you can use them:

El pasante = The intern

La pasante = The intern

El malabarista = The juggler

La malabarista = The juggler

El gerente = The manager

La gerente = The manager

El aristócrata = The aristocrat

La aristócrata = The aristocrat

In the above list, the noun endings stay the same and they are fitted for both genders, male and female. You can use these words to talk about a female or male subject and the clue to gender will be only in the article: el/la, un/una.

To put it in other words:

Tim is an intern: Tim es un pasante

Jennifer is an intern: Jennifer es una pasante

But there are other nouns that must change in order to agree with the gender of the person/animal they refer to. This is the case of nouns that refer to people, for example, relatives, member of the family, some professions and occupations, and also nouns that designate animals. Compare the following lists:

Masculine / Feminine
El oso   (male bear) / la osa (female bear)

El perro (male dog) / la perra (female dog)

El gato (male cat) / la gata (female cat)

El tigre (tiger) / la tigresa (tigress)

El león   (lion) / la leona (lioness)

El abuelo (grandfather) / la abuela (grandmother)

El primo (male cousin) / la prima (female cousin)

El tío (uncle) / la tía (aunt)

El jefe (male boss) / la jefa (female boss)

El arquitecto (male architect) / la arquitecta (female architect)

El abogado (male lawyer) / la abogada (female lawyer)

El vendedor (salesman) / la vendedora (saleswoman)

This list includes some common nouns for people and animals. You will notice that a definite or indefinite article must coincide with the noun gender. In other words, if you are using el/un, you need to use a masculine noun, or a neutral noun (i.e. those that do not have a distinguishable ending for masculine or feminine forms); and if you use la/una, you will want to follow that with a feminine noun, or a neutral one.

Number and Collective Nouns

One simple way to make a noun plural is by adding –s at the end. You can do this with nouns that end in a vowel, whether it is –a, -e, or –o. Take a look at these examples:

El oso = The bear

Los osos = The bears

La pluma = The feather

Las plumas = The feathers

La pelota = The ball

Las pelotas = The balls

El perro = The dog

Los perros = The dogs

Many nouns end in a consonant. You can make them plural by simply adding –es at the end of the word:

La virtud > Virtue

Las virtudes = The virtues

El vendedor = The salesman

Los vendedores = The salesmen

La flor = The flower

Las flores = The flowers

La mansión = The manor

Las mansiones = The manors

Notice the last example:

La mansión – las mansiones

When the noun ends in –ión, the rule applies and you need to add –es at the end of the word. However, you will need to leave out the written accent.

La canción – las canciones = The song – The songs

La decisión – las decisiones = The decision – The decisions

The last rule that you need to learn about how to form plurals is the one that applies to nouns ending in –z. Now, there not too many nouns that end in –z, but when making their plural form, you need to drop the –z, and add –ces. Here are some examples:

El antifaz = The mask

Los antifaces = The masks

La actriz = The actress

Las actrices = The actresses

La raíz = The root

Las raíces = The roots

Mixed Gender Groups

The issue of gender for nouns in Spanish may raise questions regarding, for example, how to talk about a group of people or animals when it is made up of both, male and female subjects.

Let's imagine there is a meeting at the office and people are sitting at different tables.

The secretaries are sitting around one of the tables. They are all women, so the right words would be: Las secretarias.

The managers are sitting at a different table. There are 3 women and 4 men in this group. The way you will want to refer to them is: Los gerentes

At another table we find the account managers. There are 4 women and 1 man in this group. In Spanish you need to use: Los ejecutivos de cuentas.

And the two managing directors are sitting at another table, at the front of the room. Both of them are men, so you need to use: Los directores.

To sum up, when the group is mixed you will need to use the masculine form, regardless of how many men or women there are in the group. When a group is entirely comprised of women (or female elements); you will need to use the feminine form. Similarly, when a group is made up of males, you will want to use the male form of the noun and article.

Definite and Indefinite Articles: Plural Forms

By now you already know how to use the articles in Spanish to talk about people and things. To express "*the*" you can use *el* or *la*, and to say "a/an" you use un or una.

Let's now take a look at how to use the plural forms of the definite and indefinite articles. In English, this is quite simple, because "the" is used for both, singular and plural nouns:

The flower

The flowers

And to use an indefinite article, the option is commonly "some" for plural nouns. In Spanish, however, you will have to learn the feminine and masculine forms used for plural nouns. These are fairly simple to remember, and in this lesson you will find a number or examples to help you out:

Los niños = The kids

Las sillas = The chairs

Unas flores = Some flowers

Unos perros = Some dogs

The word used for "some" is unos or unas, depending on the noun gender; las and los are used to express plural "the".

Here are some additional examples of the use of la/las/el/los:

La ciudad = The city

Las ciudades = The cities

La oficina = The office

Las oficinas = The offices

La calle = The street

Las calles = The streets

El coche = The car

Los coches = The cars

El vendedor = The salesman

Los vendedores = The salesmen

El niño = The boy

Los niños = The boys

Here are some examples of the use of un/una/unos/unas

Un mapa = A map

Unos mapas = Some maps

Un autobús = A bus

Unos autobuses = Some buses

Un río = A river

Unos ríos = Some rivers

Una vaca = A cow

Unas vacas = Some cows

Una casa = A house

Unas casas = Some houses

Una nube = A cloud

Unas nubes = Some clouds

This is easy, right? Let's revise the rules we just shared: when you want to talk about a specific person, animal or thing, you will need to use el/la/los/las. But when you want to refer to an unspecified person, animal or thing, you will want to use un/una/unos/unas.

Are these the only words you can use to talk about an unspecified thing or person? The answer is no; just like in English, you can use the equivalent of "a few", "many", "few" (more about this on the chapter for measures and quantity).

Algunos – algunas = Some, a few

Pocos – pocas = few

Muchos – muchas = many

Collective Nouns

Some words can be used to describe a group of people, animals, or things. We are talking about collective nouns. For example, when you want to talk about a group of birds, you use "a flock" in English. Let's take a look at some of these collective nouns in Spanish:

Una bandada (de pájaros) = A flock of birds

Un cardúmen (de peces) = A shoal

Un equipo (de personas) = A team

Una flota (de barcos, aviones) = A fleet

Una jauría (de perros) = A pack

Una manada (de elefantes) = A herd

Una muchedumbre (de gente) = A crowd

Un rebaño (de ovejas) = A flock of sheep

Subject Pronouns

Subject pronouns are one of the main elements in a sentence. In English, subject pronouns are essential for building a sentence, but during this lesson, you will learn that this is not true for Spanish, where pronouns can be omitted or can be "hidden" in the verb.

First, let's see what we are talking about when we say subject pronouns.

In English, the terms I, You, He, She, It, We, They are subject pronouns. We use them to conjugate verbs, to answer questions and to talk about the world around us. To start making sentences in Spanish, learning the subject pronouns is a good place to start.

Yo = I

Tú = You

Él = He

Ella = She

Nosotros = We

Ustedes = You

Ellos = They

There are some special aspects about the Spanish language that are worth mentioning.

1. The subject pronoun She = Ella does not "officially" exist in the list that children learn at school, although in everyday usage it is just as common as He = Él.

This is somehow related to another aspect of the Spanish language, which is the issue of gender. For the plural subjects We and They, Spanish speakers have two variations: feminine and masculine. Take a look:

Nosotros (We – masculine)

Nosotras (We – feminine)

Ellos (They – masculine)

Ellas (They – feminine)

The plural feminine forms, Nosotras and Ellas, can be used to refer to a group of people where all members are women. Otherwise, for mixed gender groups, the all-encompassing masculine form is used.

2. The use of the form "Vosotros". This word is equivalent to "you" (plural), and is used mostly in Spain. While Spanish speakers in the Americas recognize this word and fully understand it, they use "Ustedes" instead. You can say this is a regional aspect, so when visiting Mexico or South America, make sure you use this common form, Ustedes. Also, notice that the subject "Vosotros" requires certain variations in conjugation that are not necessary present in the use of "Ustedes". Just for reference, take a look at the following example:

You (plural) are very kind

Ustedes *son* muy amables

Vosotros *sois* muy amables

We will focus on the Spanish as spoken in Latin America, and I recommend that if you are interested in learning more about the use of Vosotros, go ahead and look up Castilian Spanish or European Spanish in any search engine.

3. The use of Usted vs Tú. If you are slightly familiar with the Spanish language, you may have heard that there is a formal and an informal way of addressing somebody. This is where Usted and Tú walk in. Both Usted and Tú mean *you* in Spanish, but depending on the context and the person you are addressing, you will want to use one or the other.

Tú (notice that it takes a written accent), is informal, it is more familiar: it's what you would use to address a person that you know well, such as a friend, your brother, your mom, a classmate, or a co-worker.

Usted is formal, and it indicates that you respect the person you are addressing. You will want to use this form when talking with a doctor, a police officer, your boss, an older person, or anybody that you are not familiar with. It is not necessarily a question of age. Even when speaking with another person on the same age range as you, you may want to use "Usted" to show respect, or to maintain a polite distance.

So, here is a quick list:

You want to be informal: Tú

You want to be formal: Usted

Interesting fact! – If you go to Argentina, more specifically to Buenos Aires, you will hear them use "vos". This is a colloquial term that replaces Tú, and is used in all the same informal situations as its more "Latin" sibling. Some other changes to verb morphology apply as well (i.e. the way a word is written), but they probably deserve a whole book of their own!

Focus on Usage: YOU may not always be necessary?

We have yet to talk about verbs, verb conjugation, and more. But in the issue of subject pronouns, there is one little aspect of the Spanish language that makes it all the more interesting: You may not always be necessary. And not just you, but I, She, He, etc. In fact, most of the time no subject is necessary at all! Are you surprised? Here is the truth behind this bold statement.

In Spanish, the subject pronoun can often be omitted, or in other words, hidden in the verb. Because the conjugation of verbs is quite particular for each subject, in speech it is easy for a trained ear to discover who the subject is without the speaker mentioning it. It is as if you had two aunts. Aunt Julia makes a delicious apple pie, it is her signature pie, and Aunt Marie makes an exquisite strawberry pie. Just by having a bite at the pie, you know if it is strawberry or apple, you know whether Aunt Julia or Aunt Marie came to visit, without even seeing them! This is a silly example to show you that the same thing happens with verb conjugations, they "hide" the subject in them. Here is a more practical example:

He writes a letter

a. Él escribe una carta

b. Escribe una carta

In letter a, the subject is evident. The subject pronoun is written in the sentence. But letter b has exactly the same meaning. What happened? The subject He = Él is already implied in the conjugation of the verb "escribir" = "to write", with the ending –e (more about this in subsequent chapters). While the writer may want to clarify who is writing the letter, this is not completely necessary, as the verb already indicates that the hidden subject is He = Él.

But, how can we be sure that the subject is He = Él? Many times this will depend on the context of communication. Sentences don't simply come flying at us, there is always a context. Maybe we have been talking about a certain person or situation before. If you are at an exam, and this sentence appears without a context, the examiners will often take this into account in case there is more than one correct answer.

When we learn more about verbs and how to conjugate them, you will see that Él (He), Ella (She) and Usted (You, singular, formal) often share the same conjugation. In the above sentence, the hidden subject may have been Él, Ella, or Usted. The answer will depend on the context. In other words, if this sentence is part of a conversation, where somebody was talking about Paul, who was at his room, sitting at his desk, the hidden subject will likely be Paul, or Él:

Paul writes a letter

Paul escribe una carta

Él escribe una carta

Escribe una carta

All of the above examples are correct.

How to Match Names and Subject Pronouns

At the beginning, it is quite useful to remember that you can often replace names with subject pronouns, and vice versa:

Anna eats ice-cream

Anna come helado

Ella come helado

Whenever you have a subject pronoun, you can replace it with a name, or names, to make a text or speech more interesting, and to avoid repetition. Here are some examples:

Bárbara – Ella

Oscar – Él

Bárbara y Oscar – Ellos

Nicolás, Eduardo y Liliana – Ellos

Liliana y Sabrina – Ellas

Yo, Liliana y Eduardo – Nosotros

Tú, Nicolás y Bárbara – Ustedes

Replacing a name with the subject pronoun or vice versa is quite useful both in writing and in speech.

As you may have noticed, there are quite a few similarities between English and Spanish when it comes to subject pronouns, which make it really easy to understand.

In terms of formality, if you are unsure whether to use "Tú" or "Usted", start with the latter, and then ask if you can use "Tú" instead. In most cases, people will agree to this!

All About Adjectives

What are adjectives? How can you identify an adjective? In a previous section, we described what an adjective is and its function within a sentence. Adjectives describe nouns; they refer to size, color, shape, weight, and other characteristics that may be visible or hidden in a noun.

Examples of adjectives in English are: big – blue – round – heavy – beautiful – talkative – intelligent, and more.

There are adjectives to describe all sorts of things, people, animals, and places. Some of them are very specific. I will provide you with a list of adjectives as used for each category. But right now, let's take a look at what makes adjectives in Spanish different from their English counterparts.

The issue of noun gender in Spanish is essential and by rule, it encompasses changes in other words in order to match the noun gender. Adjectives in Spanish change their endings according to gender, but not all of them need to change. Let's go over some of the most common adjectives, and how to make them agree in gender and number with the noun they modify.

Nouns in Spanish are either feminine or masculine. As a general rule, we said that most nouns ending in –o or –e are masculine, while most nouns ending in –a are feminine. Adjectives will follow this rule, so for masculine nouns adjectives will end in –o, and for feminine nouns, adjectives will end in –a. Here are some examples to clarify this concept:

The little boy

El niño pequeño

The little girl

La niña pequeña

The fast car

El auto rápido

The beautiful woman

La mujer bella

The heavy book

El libro pesado

Once again, thinking about gender in adjectives can be tough for native English speakers, as there is no such concept in English adjectives. Luckily, there are rules that you can easily follow to learn Spanish adjectives and how to use them properly.

1. Many common adjectives end in –o or –a depending on the noun they modify.

Expensive = Caro (masculine) / Cara (feminine)

Pretty = Lindo (masculine) / Linda (feminine)

Boring = Aburrido (masculine) / Aburrida (feminine)

Funny = Chistoso (masculine) / Chistosa (feminine)

Old = Viejo (masculine) / Vieja (feminine)

In most cases, the ending of a noun will match the ending of the adjective (the vowel that indicates gender):

Gat**o** pequeñ**o**

Cas**a** viej**a**

Libr**o** pesad**o**

But nouns can also end in –e, -ción, -ma, etc. In this case, you can decide which ending the adjective will take depending on the article that precedes the noun:

El mapa Viej**o** = The old map

La canción nueva = The new song

El clima frí**o** = The cold weather

Un diente rot**o** = A broken teeth

The issue of gender in nouns and adjectives is quite important, so take your time to go over these lessons again whenever you need to. A native Spanish speaker will still understand you even if you don't get the noun or adjective gender right the first time, but after all, you are looking to master the basics of the language, so go ahead and practice until you reach your level of comfort.

2. Adjectives that end in –e do not change for feminine or masculine nouns. They stay the same and only change to agree in number (use –s at the end to form plurals)

The brave girl = La chica valiente

The brave boy = El chico valiente

The hot soup = La sopa caliente

The hot oven = El horno caliente

Some other adjectives in this list include:

Grande = Big

Fuerte = Strong

Interesante = Interesting

Triste = Sad

Importante = Important

Horrible = Horrible

Excelente = Excelent

Visible = Visible

Inteligente = Intelligent

Example:

El libro excelent**e** = **La** novela excelent**e**

The excellent book = The excellent novel

3. Many adjectives in Spanish end in a consonant, such as –l, -r, -d, -n. These adjectives do not change for feminine or masculine nouns. However, you will need to add –es to make them plural (more about this in a minute). The list includes:

Fácil = Easy

Joven = Young

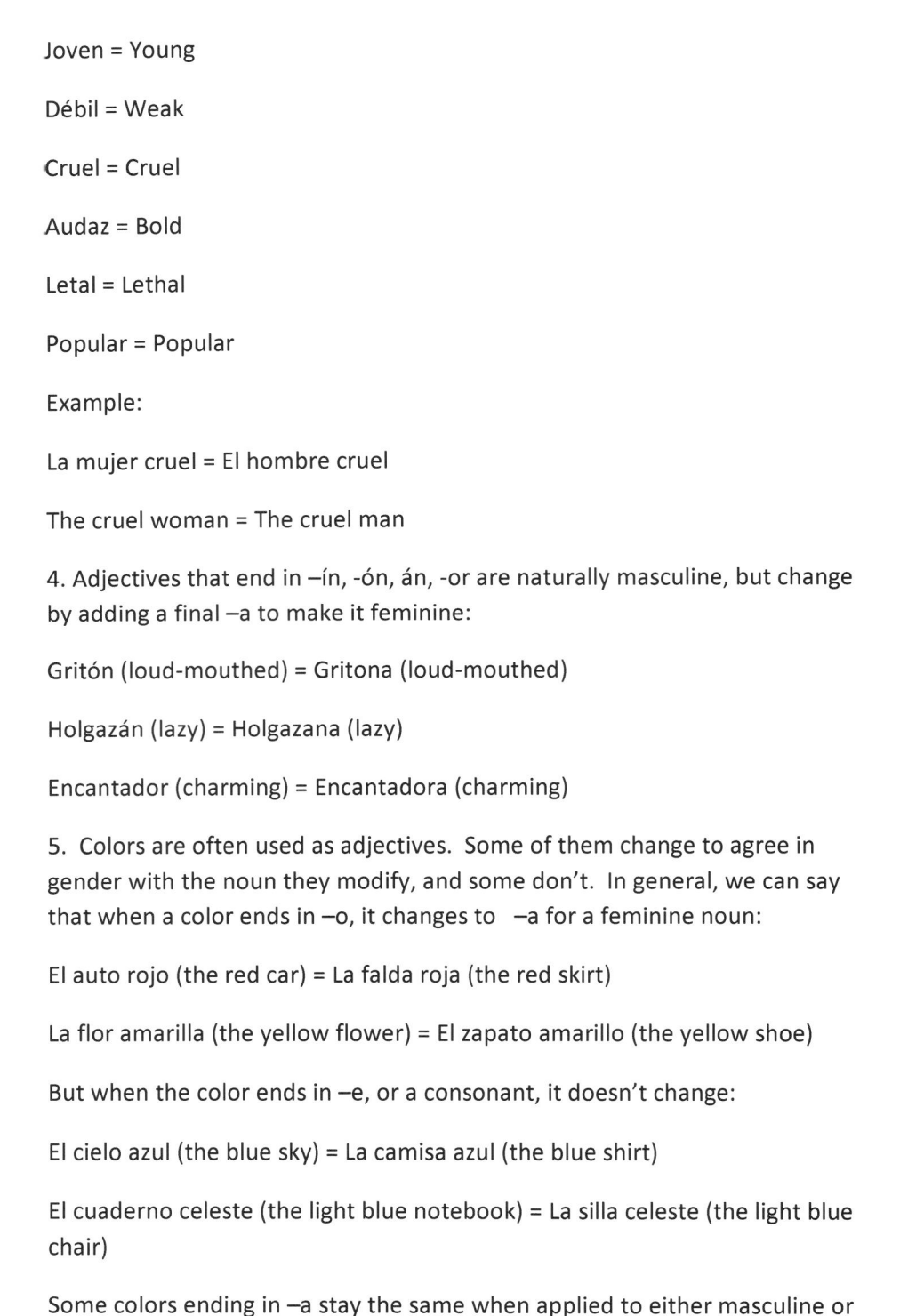

Débil = Weak

Cruel = Cruel

Audaz = Bold

Letal = Lethal

Popular = Popular

Example:

La mujer cruel = El hombre cruel

The cruel woman = The cruel man

4. Adjectives that end in –ín, -ón, án, -or are naturally masculine, but change by adding a final –a to make it feminine:

Gritón (loud-mouthed) = Gritona (loud-mouthed)

Holgazán (lazy) = Holgazana (lazy)

Encantador (charming) = Encantadora (charming)

5. Colors are often used as adjectives. Some of them change to agree in gender with the noun they modify, and some don't. In general, we can say that when a color ends in –o, it changes to –a for a feminine noun:

El auto rojo (the red car) = La falda roja (the red skirt)

La flor amarilla (the yellow flower) = El zapato amarillo (the yellow shoe)

But when the color ends in –e, or a consonant, it doesn't change:

El cielo azul (the blue sky) = La camisa azul (the blue shirt)

El cuaderno celeste (the light blue notebook) = La silla celeste (the light blue chair)

Some colors ending in –a stay the same when applied to either masculine or feminine nouns:

El vaso naranja (the orange glass) = La casa naranja (the orange house)

El auto violeta (the violet car) = La caja violeta (the violet box)

6. Adjectives of nationality change to agree with the noun. If the adjective ends in consonant, such as –l, -n, -m, add –a to form the feminine:

Alemán (German) = Alemana (German)

Catalán = Catalana

Francés = Francesa

Finlandés = Finlandesa

If the adjective ends in –o, it changes to –a to form the feminine:

Americano = Americana

Australiano = Australiana

Chino = China

Some nationality adjectives end in –se. They do no change to agree with gender:

Ella es canadiense = Él es canadiense

Ella es costarricense = Él es costarricense

7. Adjectives ending in –erior do not change according to gender. They only have one form that is used for both, feminine and masculine nouns. Also adjectives ending in –z do not change:

Superior (Superior)

Interior (Interior/Internal)

Exterior (External)

Anterior (Previous)

Inferior (Inferior/Lower)

Feliz (Happy)

Adjectives: Number

During this lesson, I told you a few details about how to make some adjectives plural. This is again a new concept for speakers of English, as this rule does not apply to their language. In Spanish, adjectives not only need to agree in gender with the noun, they also need to agree in number. If the noun is in the plural, the adjective will have to be too.

Let's go over some of the rules for forming plural adjectives.

For adjectives ending in –o, -a, or –e, simply add –s to make them plural:

Lindo = Lindos

Nueva = Nuevas

Inteligente = Inteligentes

Or,

Bueno = Buena = Buenos = Buenas

Most adjectives that end in consonant take –es to form the plural:

Fácil (Easy) = Fáciles

Holgazán (Lazy) = Holgazanes

Joven (Young) = Jóvenes

Adjectives that end in –z will change z by c and add –es:

Feli**z** = Feli**ces**

Finally, adjectives that end in –or, án, ín, or –on TAKE –es or –as TO FORM THE PLURAL. The ending –es will form the plural of the masculine, and –as will form the plural of the feminine:

Un hombre encantad**or** = Unos hombres encantad**ores**

Una mujer encantad**ora** = Unas mujeres encantad**oras**

Position of Adjectives within a Sentence

In general, adjectives follow the noun, in other words, they are placed after the noun in a sentence:

La habitación (grande y luminosa) = The big, bright room

El auto (viejo, desgastado y sucio) = The old, worn out, dirty car

Sometimes, the adjective can be placed before the noun for emphasis:

El viejo Molino = The old mill

Finally, when the adjective indicates an intrinsic characteristic of the noun, as in something that is within its nature, it is placed before the noun, and it doesn't add information about it:

La fría nieve = The cold snow

El azul cielo = The blue sky

Want to know even more about adjectives in Spanish? When more than one adjective are used for a single noun, they appear separated by a comma (,):

El vestido rojo, viejo, corto e inservible = The red, short, old and useless dress

When an adjective describes two or more nouns, it takes the plural form:

El sillón y el cuadro modernos = The modern painting and couch

La falda y la blusa amarillas = The yellow top and skirt

When an adjective describes two nouns with different gender, the masculine form is used:

La mesa y el sillón modernos = The modern table and couch

Positive and Negative Adjective

This list of common adjectives will help you get started when you need to describe something in terms of positive and negative aspects. This list

Includes adjectives for describing people, animals, things, places, and abstract nouns.

Positive Adjectives

Bueno (good)

Lindo (cute)

Fino (refined)

Tranquilo (quiet)

Inteligente (intelligent)

Fácil (easy)

Genial (great)

Hermoso (beautiful)

Joven (young)

Generoso (generous)

Verdadero (true)

Bello (nice, beautiful)

Feliz (happy)

Excelente (Excellent)

Agradable (nice, appealing)

Bonito (cute)

Limpio (clean)

Correcto (correct)

Importante (important)

Útil (useful)

Afortunado (lucky)

Seguro (safe)

Respetuoso (respectful)

Cortés (polite)

Amable (kind)

Adorable (adorable)

Rico (tasty, yummy)

Delicioso (delicious)

Lujoso (luxurious)

Ordenado (tidy, organized)

Justo (fair, just)

Divertido (fun)

Emocionante (exciting)

Negative Adjectives
Lento (slow)

Malo (bad)

Caro (expensive)

Ruidoso (noisy)

Pesado (heavy)

Difícil (difficult)

Peligroso (dangerous)

Tarde (late)

Oscuro (dark)

Aburrido (boring)

Desafortunado (unlucky)

Pobre (poor)

Tacaño (mean)

Feo (ugly)

Triste (sad)

Terrible (terrible)

Desagradable (unpleasant)

Sucio (dirty)

Horrible (horrible)

Equivocado (wrong)

Agresivo (agressive)

Corrupto (corrupt)

Injusto (unfair)

More and More Adjectives

With the following lists, you will never run out of ways to describe everything that is around you. Because adjectives make up an important part of speech, here are some groups that will help you express your opinion about things like people, places, animals, clothes, and more. Some adjectives may appear in more than one category.

Adjectives for describing people

Alto (tall)

Bajo (short)

Esbelto (fit)

Robusto (sturdy)

Gordo (fat)

Delgado (slim, thin)

Joven (young)

Fuerte (strong)

Viejo (old)

Maduro (mature)

Elegante (elegant)

Desordenado (messy)

Sucio (dirty)

Amable (kind)

Simpático (nice, outgoing)

Cariñoso (loving)

Sensible (sensitive)

Caritativo (giving, charitable)

Generoso (generous, giving)

Honesto (honest)

Vago (lazy)

Cobarde (cowardly)

Valiente (brave)

Irresponsable (irresponsible)

Violento (violent)

Grosero (rude)

Egoísta (selfish)

Pesado (annoying)

Malvado (mean, evil)

Cordial (warm, cordial)

Mentiroso (liar)

Desagradable (appaling, unpleasant)

Trabajador (hard working)

Inteligente (intelligent)

Sincero (honest, sincere)

Honrado (honorable)

Educado (polite)

Encantador (charming)

Responsable (resposible)

Creativo (creative)

Adjectives for Describing Animals

Salvaje (wild)

Doméstico (domestic)

Agresivo (aggresive)

Ágil (agile)

Tranquilo (quiet)

Grande (big, large)

Pequeño (tiny, small)

Carnívoro (carnivorous)

Herbívoro (herbivorous)

Peludo (furry)

Veloz (fast)

Feroz (fierce, ferocious)

Peligroso (dangerous)

Manso (tame, quiet)

Venenoso (poisonous)

De cuatro patas (four-legged)

Volador (flying)

Colorido (colorful)

Suave (soft)

Ruidoso (noisy)

Adjectives for Describing Movies and Entertainment

Emocionante (thrilling, exciting)

Aburrido (boring, dull)

Largo (long)

Corto (short, brief)

Costoso (expensive)

Barato (inexpensive)

Intenso (intense)

Dramático (dramatic)

Escalofriante (terrifying)

Aventurero (adventurous)

Chistoso (funny)

Realista (realistic)

Infantil (childish)

Fascinante (fascinating)

Adjectives for Describing a House

Espaciosa (spacious)

Grande (large, big)

Luminosa (bright, luminous)

Moderna (modern)

Antigua (old)

Mediana (average, medium-sized)

Amoblada (furnished)

Costosa (expensive)

Económica (cheap, inexpensive)

Angosta (narrow)

Ancha (wide)

Oscura (dark)

Ruidosa (noisy)

Cómoda (comfortable)

Atractiva (attractive)

Ecléctica (eclectic)

Fría (cold)

Ventilada (airy)

Excéntrica (eccentric)

Tradicional (traditional)

Acogedora (cozy)

Lujosa (luxurious)

Bien conservado (well-maintained)

Segura (safe, secure)

Enorme (huge)

Adjectives for Describing Jobs and Professions

Aburrido (boring)

Emocionante (exciting)

Ecléctico (eclectic)

Difícil (hard)

Fácil (easy)

Inspirador (inspiring)

Creativo (creative)

Cambiante (always changing)

Peligroso (dangerous)

Seguro (secure, safe)

Possessive Adjectives

We use possessive adjectives to express ownership. In other words, we use these adjectives to say who the owner of something is, or to whom something belongs. You use possessive adjectives in English all the time, look at them now:

My – Your – His – Her – Its – Our – Their

Now in Spanish, as usual, there are some variations to take into account. Remember that we said the issue of gender affects many aspects of the language? Possessive adjectives are no exception. Some of them show variation in number depending on the noun, and some will also vary according to the noun gender. The gender or number of the person(s) that own the noun are not important. Here is the complete list of possessive adjectives in Spanish:

Mi – my

Tu – your

Su – her/his

Nuestro – our

Su – your (plural)

Su – their

As you have noticed, "Su" is used for more than one subject. In general, the context will provide the necessary information to know who this word represents. Otherwise there are additional words that can be used to clarify. We will get back to this in a minute.

Read the following examples:

Mi casa es bonita = My house is pretty

Mis botas son negras = My boots are black

Tu perro es fiel = Your dog is loyal

Tus notas están bien = Your grades are ok

Su hermano es abogado = Her/His brother is a lawyer

Sus hermanas están en Canadá = Her/His sisters are in Canada

Earlier we mentioned that possessive adjectives in Spanish have variations to agree with number and gender of the noun they modify. The above sentences show the first case. These three adjectives, Mi, Tu, and Su have two forms: singular and plural. If the noun they precede is singular, they will stay the same. If they modify a plural noun (like sisters, grades, boots, etc.), they will take –s at the end to form the plural.

Mi gato = My cat

Mis gatos = My cats

Su pastel = Her pie

Sus pasteles = Her pies

Mi, Tu, and Su do not change to agree with the noun gender, only to agree with number (singular or plural)

However, the adjective "Nuestro = Our" has four variations to agree with number and gender of the noun it modifies. Here are the details:

Nuestro (masculine, singular) = Nuestros (masculine, plural)

Nuestra (feminine, singular) = Nuestras (feminine, plural)

Remember that possessive adjectives agree with the noun they modify, not with the "possessor" (the person that owns that noun). Here are some examples to clarify this concept:

Mariana, Lucía, and Marta own a male cat. They say "our cat", or in Spanish:

Nuestro gato

See how they use the singular (one cat) and masculine (male cat) form of the adjective: Nuestro.

Mariana, Lucía, and Marta also own a table. They say "our table", or in Spanish:

Nuestra mesa

Because it is a single object (one table), and in Spanish it is a feminine noun (la mesa):

Nuestra

If the noun possessed is plural, they will use nuestros or nuestras, depending on the noun gender:

Nuestr**os** libr**os** = Our books

Nuestr**as** plant**as** = Our plants

The use of "Su"

The possessive adjective Su is used for all of these subjects:

Su – Él = His

Su – Ella = Her

Su – Usted = Your (formal)

Su – de ello = Its

Su – Ellos = Their

Look at the following examples:

Su casa está cerca = His house is nearby

Su casa está cerca = Her house is nearby

Su casa está cerca = Your (formal) house is nearby

Su casa está cerca = Their house is nearby

Looking at the above examples, you may feel uncertain about how to decide which subject the speaker is referring to. Whose house is nearby? In most cases, that information can be found in the context. In other words, if you are reading a story or participating in a conversation, this sentence will be part of a series of facts that will be provided. Certainly, if the conversation was about your new classmate, Adriana, or a co-worker, José, you will be able to infer who that "Su" refers to.

When there is not enough information in the context, additional words, and phrases can be used to convey the intended meaning:

La casa de él está cerca = His house is nearby

La casa de ella está cerca = Her house is nearby

La casa de usted está cerca = Your (formal) house is nearby

La casa de ellos está cerca = Their house is nearby

To make it simpler:

Su (de él) = His

Su (de ella) = Her

Su (de usted) = Your (formal)

Su (de ello) = Its

Su (de ellos) = Their

A special note about the Castilian "Vuestro"

Vuestro = Your is a form of the possessive adjective used primarily in Spain. As we mentioned before, Castilian Spanish differs slightly from the Spanish spoken in the Americas. Similarly to Nuestro = Our, this adjective has four variations:

Vuestro = Vuestros

Vuestra = Vuestras

Just like with Nuestro, it changes to agree in number and gender with the noun it modifies. The English equivalent is always the same: Your (plural).

Comparisons

Often times, we need to describe something or define something by using comparisons. In English, we can do this by using the structure more... than, and less... than. We will now learn how to make comparisons in Spanish, what aspects can be compared, and how to choose the right verb for comparing.

The first type of comparison we are going to look at is the case where there is inequality:

Susan is more intelligent than I

Fred is younger than you

Peter has less money than Tim

To make comparisons of inequity, we can take three aspects into consideration: adjectives (intelligent, young), nouns (money, brothers) and adverbs (fast, efficiently).

Let's start with adjectives. A simple structure that you can use in Spanish is as follows:

Más / menos + adjective + que

It is quite similar to its English counterpart: more/less + adjective + than. Take a look at these examples:

Bárbara es más atractiva que Emilia = Barbara is more attractive than Emilia

Cancún es más caluroso que Roma = Cancun is hotter than Rome

In Spanish, the words you need to use are always más/menos.... que. Unlike the English formula where you can add –er at the end of an adjective to form the comparison, Spanish does not have this feature, and the standard más/menos .... que is always used.

Buenos Aires es menos moderna que Nueva York = Buenos Aires is less modern than New York

Now that you have a good knowledge of how to make comparisons, let's move on to comparing nouns.

The difference with nouns is that instead of using the verb Ser = To be, you will need to use the verb Tener = To have. Another possible variation is to use the verb Haber = There are. Why is this necessary? Because nouns in comparison are often related to possession or availability. Look at the following examples:

Tengo más cuadernos que Laura = I have more notebooks than Laura

Hay más gatos aquí que en el jardín = There are more cats here than in the garden

Ella tiene menos hermanas que yo = She has less sisters than I

Comparatives and Numbers

Sometimes, the comparative is used to express quantities, in excess (more than) or in need (less than). When a number follows the comparative, you will need to use "de" instead of "que". Here are some examples:

Hay más de treinta países en esa region = There are more than thirty countries in that region

Ella tiene menos de cinco años de experiencia = She has less than five years of experience

In the examples above, the comparison is not between two elements, but rather between something and a target number. Remember: use "de" before numbers to express comparisons.

Comparing Adverbs

Many adverbs in Spanish end in –mente. This feature makes them quite easy to identify and to compare. You will need to use the same structure: más/menos .... que. Here are some examples:

Ella canta más suavemente que Paulina = She sings more softly than Paulina

Elias trabaja menos eficientemente que yo = Elias works less efficiently than I

The second type of comparison we are going to learn is comparison of equity. We talk about equity when the two things we want to compare have similar characteristics. In English, we will use the structure as .... as. Take a look:

This house is as big as mine

Kevin is as old as my brother

In Spanish, this comparison takes the form of tan.... como. This structure can be used for adjectives and adverbs. Here is how:

Patricia es tan inteligente como Adriana = Patricia is as intelligent as Adriana

Este auto es tan rápido como el mío = This car is as fast as mine

José trabaja tan eficientemente como Alicia = Jose works as efficiently as Alicia

Now, comparing nouns is a little different in Spanish. Instead of using the word tan... como, you will want to use the following variations:

Tanto ..(noun).. como

Tanta .. (noun).. como

Tantos .. (noun).. como

Tantas .. (noun).. como

As you may have already guessed, the word Tanto needs to agree with the noun gender and number. Here are some examples to clarify this point:

En esta calle hay tantos restaurantes como cafeterias = There are as many restaurants in this street as cafes

Él tiene tantos juguetes como su hermano = He has as many toys as his brother

Ella tiene tanta fe como su madre = She has as much faith as her mother

Again, noun gender and number are essential in determining which option to use. Here is a brief reminder that you can use:

Tanto .... como = masculine, singular

Tanta .... como = feminine, singular

Tantos .... como = masculine, plural

Tantas .... como = feminine, plural

The Biggest, Largest, and Latest. Superlatives

We use superlatives to describe a noun as having a particular characteristic that puts it at the top, or at the bottom of a class or group. For example, we can say that Sally is very brave or we can say that she is the bravest girl in the group. On the other end, we can say that Jim is very short or that he is the shortest boy in the class. In both examples, we are comparing the noun's qualities with the rest of a group or we are simply stating superiority without comparing it to any group. We will now learn how to use superlatives in Spanish.

The structure for doing this in English is quite simple: we use the (definite article) + most/least + adjective. Similarly, in Spanish we need to say:

El / La + noun + más / menos + adjective + de (group or context)

Here is an example:

Ella es **la chica más bonita de** la fiesta = She is the prettiest girl in the party

Notice that at the beginning of the sentence we need to use the definite article. It will need to match the noun that we are describing. Remember definite articles are:

El

La

Los

Las

Remember that the definite article serves to identify clearly the noun we are talking about.

Rita **es la chica más bonita** de la fiesta = Rita is the prettiest girl in the party

Sometimes you will come across sentences where the noun is absent. This is perfectly correct, and the meaning is the same:

Juan es el hombre menos afortunado del mundo = Juan is the least fortunate man in the world.

In the above example, the word hombre = man can be omitted. The resulting sentence would look like this:

Juan es el menos afortunado del mundo = Juan is the least fortunate in the world

Other contexts of superlatives may include:

Del mundo = In the world

Del barrio = In the neighborhood

De la clase = In the class

De mi familia = In my family

Del equipo = In the team

Del país = In the country

Que conozco = That I know

Examples:

Diana es la chica más honesta que conozco = Diana is the most honest girl I know

José es el miembro menos atlético de la familia = José is the least athletic member of the family

Other Ways of Expressing the Superlative

You can also use other words and phrases to express the superlative, without comparing the noun to a group or context. What if you need to say that somebody or something is the most ... (period)? You do not have a context of reference, you simply want to convey that the noun is the "best" or the "worst". Here are some ways to do that in Spanish. Let's start with the easy ones:

El mejor – La mejor – Los mejores – Las mejores = The best

El peor – La peor – Los peores – Las peores = The worst

Notice that in the above phrases, the four options correspond with noun gender and number (feminine, masculine, plural, singular).

Other words you can use in this category. Add an adjective following these words:

Muy = Very

Extremadamente = Extremely

Totalmente = Totally

Completamente = Completely

The form –ísimo / -ísima / -ísimos / -ísimas:

Aburridísimo = (Superlative of boring)

Asustadísimo = (Superlative of scared)

Emocionadísimas = (Superlative of excited)

Here are some examples to clarify this point:

Él es completamente fascinante = Hé is absolutely fascinating

La profesora estaba emocionadísima = The teacher was incredibly excited

The above examples express the superlative without really comparing it with a group or context. It simply states a fact using extreme adjectives.

So, the two most important things you need to remember about superlatives are:

* You can use them to compare a specific noun's characteristic with a group or context;

* You can use them to state a fact using extreme adjectives

Affirmative, Negative, and Interrogative Sentences

Every sentence can be classified as an affirmative statement, a negation or a question. Throughout the previous lessons, we have seen a number of examples in the affirmative:

Ella es abogada = She is a lawyer

Mi hermana está en Canadá = My sister is in Canada

Soy de Brazil = I'm from Brazil

In affirmative statements, the subject may be present (Ella, Mi hermana), or it can be omitted (hidden in the conjugated verb, as in "soy"). You can use the following formula to make sentences in the affirmative:

(subject) + verb + object/complement

(Nosotros) somos amigos = We are friends

In the example above, the subject "nosotros" appears within brackets because, as you already know, it can be omitted.

Negative Statements

Forming the negative in Spanish is quite simple. Unlike English, where you need an auxiliary and also the verb may change, the Spanish forms the negative by simply adding the word "no" before the verb. Take a look at these examples:

Ella no quiere estudiar = She doesn't want to study

No soy puntual = I'm not punctual

When the main verb in a sentence is the verb Ser = To be, the word "no" is placed right before Ser, and this is followed by an adjective, an adverb, etc.

When the main verb in a sentence is a common verb (such as decir, querer, salir, etc.), the negative word "no" is placed before the main verb, and this may be followed by another verb, a noun, etc.

María no quiere hablar (no + main verb + a second verb) = Maria doesn't want to talk

Elías no quiere helado (no + main verb + noun) = Elias doesn't want ice-cream

The main verb needs to be conjugated, just like in affirmative statements:

María quiere hablar

María **no** quiere hablar

Answering questions with the negative

When the answer to a question is in the negative, you will need to use a second negative word. Something similar is used in English:

Do you want coffee?

No, I don't want coffee.

In Spanish, you can use a number of negative words, aside from "no", but right now let's take a look at some of the most common negative answers:

¿Eres tú abogado? = No, yo no soy abogado.

Are you a lawyer? = No, I'm not a lawyer.

¿Está María en su casa? = No, ella no está en su casa.

Is Maria at home? = No, Maria is not at home.

In these simple sentences, you can see that there is a double negation. These are examples of "complete negative answers", in other words, this is a polite way of answering. You could also just say "No", and the message would come across, but at the same time, it may sound a bit rude, unless it is part of an informal chat, where there is no need to elaborate on the answer.

¿Sabes dónde está el teatro? = No, no sé dónde está el teatro

Do you know where the theatre is? = No, I don't know

¿Eres de Colombia? = No, (yo) no soy de Colombia

Notice that in the second example, the subject Yo = I is between brackets to show a different way of expressing negation, where the subject is, again, hidden in the conjugated verb.

Other Words to Form the Negative

As we mentioned earlier, the word "No" is not the only available option to form the negative in Spanish. Similarly to English, you can use a variety of words such as never, neither, nobody, etc.

Take a look at this list before learning how to use them:

Nunca = Never

Nada = Nothing / Anything

Jamás = Never

Ningún / Ninguna = No (+ noun), None

Nadie = Nobody

Sometimes these words will replace the word NO and sometimes they will add to the negative sentence by coming after the word no. Here are some examples:

¿Paula visitó tu casa? = No, Paula nunca visitó mi casa

Did Paula visit your house? = No, Paula never visited my house

¿Está Alan en el aula? = No, nadie está en el aula

Is Alan in the classroom? = No, nobody is in the classroom

These negative words not only can be used to respond to questions, you can also use them in negative statements:

Nadie juega al fútbol = Nobody plays football

Nunca como helado = I never eat ice-cream

The words nada = nothing, and ningún = no (with all 4 variations) are often found in sentences with double negation:

No hay nada en mi heladera = There is nothing in my fridge

No hay ninguna flor en mi jardín = There are no flowers in my garden

This is a common aspect of the Spanish language and one you will come across often when reading a novel or an article, etc. Multiple negations are a feature of this language.

Here are the four variations of the negative word "ninguno"

Ninguno / ningún (before a masculine, singular noun)

Ninguna (feminine, singular)

Ningunos (masculine, plural)

Ningunas (feminine, plural)

Asking Questions in Spanish

You may find this interesting and convenient: The Spanish language is quite flexible when it comes to forming questions. This will give you a certain freedom in knowing that sometimes it is possible to choose the order of words. Take a look at the following examples:

¿Está Pablo en la tienda? = Is Paul at the store?

¿Pablo está en la tienda? = Is Paul at the store?

¿Está en la tienda Pablo? = Is Paul at the store?

All of the examples above are correct, and they show that in Spanish, the order of the words in questions is not written in stone, at least in this type of questions, as we will see in a minute.

When the question has a main verb (in this case, the verb Ser = To be), and there are no question words, you have three options:

Noun + verb + object

¿Pablo está en la tienda?

Verb + noun + object

¿Está Pablo en la tienda?

Verb + object + noun

¿Está en la tienda Pablo?

One aspect worth mentioning about questions in Spanish is that they take two question marks: an opening mark (¿) and a closing mark (?). Although nowadays, in many written pieces, especially informal writings such as emails, text messages, etc., this rule seems to be in decline, in formal and academic writing, it is extremely important to maintain both opening and closing marks.

Question words in Spanish: What they are and how to use them
This is a list of the most common question words you will find in Spanish. Some of them present variations, such as adding a preposition to further define the meaning; we will see some of these variations in a moment. This list will come in handy for making all types of questions. You may want to memorize them or take them with you on your trips. An explanation on how to use them follows the list:

¿Qué? – What?

¿Cómo? – How?

¿Por qué? – Why?

¿Dónde? – Where?

¿Cuándo? – When?

¿Cuánto/a? – How much?

¿Cuantos/as? – How many?

¿Quién? – Who?

Questions words are introductory words or phrases that serve the purpose of finding specific information about something. Think about the following examples:

Does Ally study French?

The answer to this question will be YES/NO. But what if you wanted to find out more details about this fact? You will want to use questions words such as:

Where does Ally study French?

When does Ally study French?

Why does Ally study French?

And so on. Similarly, in Spanish you can find out more about something with the use of questions words. Take a look at these questions:

¿Anna vive en Suiza? = Does Anna live in Switzerland?

¿Por qué vive Anna en Suiza? = Why does Anna live in Switzerland?

¿Dónde vive Anna en Suiza exactamente? = Where exactly does Anna live in Switzerland?

¿Cuánto tiempo ha vivido Anna en Suiza? = How long has Ann lived in Switzerland?

To make questions using introductory words and phrases, you will have to invert the order of noun and verb. In other words, the measure of freedom we discussed before does not apply to questions that begin with introductory words.

Which one is correct? (The answer is marked right next to each sentence):

Where does Lucy make the cake?

¿Donde Lucy prepara la torta? (X)

¿Dónde prepara Lucy la torta? (OK)

¿Donde la torta prepara lucy? (X)

How does inversion work in Spanish questions? You will simply need to identify the <u>main verb</u>, and place the subject right after it:

¿Qué perro **tienes** (tú)? = What (kind of) dog do you have?

¿Cuántos perros **tienes** (**tú**)? = How many dogs do you have?

¿Dónde **cantarán los artistas**? = Where will the singers perform?

¿Quién **será tu padrino**? = Who will be your godfather?

¿Dónde **está mi esposa**? = Where is my wife?

¿Cuántas flores **trae Emilia**? = How many flowers does Emilia bring?

Some Variations

It is common to find certain variations that complete this list of introductory question words. Their meaning is somewhat related to the existing words, so it's important that you focus and learn them as well.

¿Quién? – Who?

¿A quién? – Whom?

¿De quién? – Whose? / From whom?

¿Con quién? – With whom?

¿Dónde? – Where?

¿De dónde? – From where?

¿Hacia dónde? – (To) Where?

¿Adónde? – To where?

¿Por qué? – Why?

To answer this question you will use: Porque = Because

Before going into tenses, A little word from the author!

How to overcome inhibitions

Many students feel awkward or inhibited when they try to speak in a foreign language. There is absolutely no reason to be afraid to sound a little strange, especially at the beginning when you are just getting started and everything is new. Think of yourself as a little child that is learning their first words. Nobody would judge a baby and blame them for not speaking correctly or pronouncing words like a university graduate. Now, we are not saying that you will sound like a baby, but you have to understand that you are most likely completely new to this language, and you need to GO THROUGH the experience to actually improve your ability to speak the language and master it. Do not try to look at it as making a mistake. Instead, think of it as a mandatory process for the mastery of the Spanish language. Do not assume that people will find it funny or criticize you because this is most likely far from reality. On the contrary, enjoy every step of finding the right way to pronounce a word, the correct way to form sentences, and the results you will get are going to be much greater.

One trick to keep in mind: if you try to keep your English sounds when you speak Spanish, you will be stuck in the border without going anywhere. If your goal is to speak Spanish, you need to let go of the English sounds and open your arms to a whole new array of words and sounds. Get out of your comfort zone and move your tongue to imitate the Spanish sounds and pronunciation. You may feel strange at first, but as you go on it will be more and more natural to "switch" from one language to the other.

The Present Tense

This is it. All the aspects that you have learned so far in this book have prepared you for this moment. This is what most students dread: conjugations and tenses. I will tell you, it is one thing to learn a few words in a language, but to really understand sentence formation, the tenses used; this is what ultimately allows you to express yourself in a language and to understand others.

There are two main aspects that you need to learn about each tense:

* How to effectively and accurately conjugate verbs, and

* When to use it.

Learning to conjugate verbs is a process that takes time and effort. Children learn by making mistakes and being corrected by their parents, but as a grown up you have other tools to help you achieve the level you desire. This book will provide you with a simple formula to conjugate each type of verb, separated into categories, indicating when something is different and pointing out the general rules. This will greatly simplify your learning process. Nevertheless, online you will find a myriad of tools and websites that will help you with conjugation when you are just trying to get started. One thing is for sure, repetition, repetition, repetition is the secret to achieving a level of comfort and to master the lessons from this book and any other online tool.

Let us start by taking a look at some verbs and how to conjugate them.

First, you need to know that there are two types of verbs: regular and irregular. We say a verb is regular when the first part of the word, the stem, doesn't change when the verb is conjugated. Let's identify each part of a verb:

Bailar (To dance)

Bail (stem) – ar (ending)

Some verbs will present variations in the stem, for example:

Verb: jugar = to play

Yo **jueg**o = I play

Tú **jueg**as = You play

Él **jueg**a = He plays

Nosotros **jug**amos = we play

Ustedes **jueg**an = You (plural) play

Ellos **jueg**an = They play

This verb is considered irregular because not all subjects present the same stem. The stem in Él is Jueg-, while the stem in Nosotros is Jug-. It is not uniform.

Regular verbs on the other hand are consistent and uniform. The stem remains the same and the only part that changes to agree with the subject is the ending of the verb.

For each tense, there will be different endings for different subjects. We are going to start by taking a look at the three types of verbs: -ar, -er, and –ir verbs.

Verbs in infinitive will take one of the endings, -ar, -er and –ir. You can follow the rules in order to conjugate them properly according to each ending. Take a look at the following example:

Verb: Cantar = To sing

Yo cant**o** = I sing

Tú cant**as** = You sing

Él cant**a** = He sings

Ella cant**a** = She sings

Nosotros cant**amos** = We sing

Ustedes cant**an** = You sing

Ellos cant**an** = They sing

Can you identify the stem and the ending in this verb? That's correct, the stem is always cant-, and the ending changes to agree with the subject.

To conjugate a verb is to change it in order to agree with the subject. This is the pattern for regular –ar verbs, using *cantar* as an example:

Verb: **cantar = to sing**

Yo {verb stem + o} = cant**o**

Tú {verb stem + as} = cant**as**

Él {verb stem + a} = cant**a**

Ella {verb stem + a} = cant**a**

Nosotros {verb stem + amos} = cant**amos**

Ustedes {verb stem + an} = cant**an**

Ellos {verb stem + an} = cant**an**

Let's take a look at how to conjugate –er verbs. Here is an example:

Verb: Romper (To break)

Yo romp**o** = I break

Tú romp**es** = You break

Él romp**e** = He breaks

Nosotros romp**emo**s = We break

Ustedes romp**en** = You (plural) break

Ellos romp**en** = They break

The above example shows that the pattern has changed slightly. The subject Yo keeps the same rule: to conjugate the verb, simply drop the –er ending and add –o. But the rest is different. For regular –er verbs, you will have to drop the ending and add one of the following, according to each subject: -es, -e, -emos, -en.

Finally, let's study the case of a regular –ir verb:

Verb: Sufrir (To suffer)

Yo sufr**o** = I suffer

Tú sufr**es** = You suffer

Él sufr**e** = He suffers

Nosotros sufr**imos** = We suffer

Ustedes sufr**en** = You (plural) suffer

Ellos sufr**en** = They suffer

Again, the subject Yo takes –o at the end, while the rest of the subjects change differently. For regular –ir verbs, you will have to drop the ending and add one of the following, according to each subject: -es, -e, -imos, -en.

Let's revise these rules briefly to clarify any doubt:

To conjugate regular verbs with –ar, -er and –ir endings for the subject Yo = I, simply drop the ending and add –o:

Infinitive: nad**ar** = to swim

Yo nad**o** = I swim

Infinitive: aprend**er** = to learn

Yo aprend**o** = I learn

Infinitive: asist**ir** = to assist

Yo asist**o** = I assist

The subject Tú = You behaves slightly different in Spanish. For verbs with –ar endings, drop the –ar and add –as. For verbs with –er and –ir endings, drop these and add –es. Here are examples of all three verb endings to clarify this concept:

Infinitive: salt**ar** = to jump

Tú salt**as** = You jump

Infinitive: aprend**er** = to learn

Tú aprend**es** = You learn

Infinitive: sub**ir** = to go up

Tú sub**es** = You go up

The subjects Él = He, Ella = She, and Usted = You (formal) present a distinctive conjugation. For verbs ending in –ar, drop the ending and add –a. For verbs ending in –er and –ir, drop the ending and add –e. These three subjects take the same conjugation, so it makes them easier to remember. Here are some examples:

Infinitive: am**ar** = to love

Él am**a** = He loves

Ella am**a** = She loves

Usted am**a** = You love

Infinitive: beb**er** = to drink

Él beb**e** = He drinks

Ella beb**e** = She drinks

Usted bebe = You (formal) drink

Infinitive: decidir = to decide

Él decide = He decides

Ella decide = She decides

Usted decide = You (formal) decide

Notice that for regular –ar, -er and –ir verbs, you only need to drop the endings and add –a and –e accordingly. It is that simple to conjugate verbs in the present.

Let's continue with the conjugation of regular verbs for the subject Nosotros = We. For regular verbs ending in –ar, drop the ending and add –amos. For verbs ending in –er you will need to drop the ending and add –emos; and for verb ending in –ir, drop the ending and add –imos. Look at how the first letter of the "add on" is the same as the vowel you drop from the infinitive.

Infinitive: trabajar = to work

Nosotros trabajamos = We work

Infinitive: esconder = to hide

Nosotros escondemos = We hide

Infinitive: permitir = to allow

Nosotros permitimos = We allow

This one is quite easy basically because of the coincidence between the ending dropped and the new ending that needs to be added on.

Now we will look at the subject Ustedes = You (plural), and Ellos = They. These two last pronouns also share the same conjugation pattern; for regular –ar verbs, drop the ending and add –an; for –er and –ir verbs, drop the ending and add –en. Here are some examples:

Infinitive: enseñar = to teach

Ustedes enseñan = You (plural) teach

Ellos enseñ**an** [They teach

Infinitive: vend**er** = to sell

Ustedes vend**en** = You (plural) sell

Ellos vend**en** = They sell

Infinitive: viv**ir** = to live

Ustedes viv**en** = You (plural) live

Ellos viv**en** = They live

Remember that the subjects Nosotros and Ellos also have a feminine variation: Nosotras and Ellas, that take the same endings that have been explained.

Now that you know how to conjugate verbs in the present tense, let's take a look at the Present Simple.

The Present Simple Tense

While the name may indicate that this tense is used for talking about actions in the present, you would be surprised to know that it has many uses, even to talk about the future! Let's take a look at the most common uses of the present simple tense.

1. We use the Present Simple to talk about a customary action, something you do regularly or repeatedly. Every day actions, routines, and regular events; they all go into this category. Here are some examples:

Sandy se levanta a las 8am. = Sandy wakes up at 8am

Ella va a la escuela a las 9 de la mañana = She goes to school at 9 in the morning

Sandy hace gimnasia todas las tardes = Sandy exercises every afternoon

These sentences express a routine, a typical day in someone's life.

2. The Present Simple can be used to describe facts and laws of nature. These facts are often called "eternal truths". Here are some examples:

El sol se oculta en el oeste = The sun sets in the west

Los bebés lloran = Babies cry

3. You can use the Present Simple to talk about events in the near future. Especially when describing an immediate and planned action in the future. Read the following examples:

Adriana llega mañana = Adriana arrives tomorrow

Se reunen el sábado por primera vez = They meet on Saturday for the first time

4. You can use the Present Simple to talk about past events, historical or personal, and to convey a sense of "recentness" or to paint a better picture of the action being related. Here are some examples:

Yo camino hacia la puerta y veo una paloma en la mesa
 walk to the door and see a pigeon on the table (depicts an image of the action being related)

El presidente firma el tratado y consigue la paz = The President signs the treaty and seals the peace.

Affirmative, Negative, and Interrogative Statements

As we mentioned before, one of the main aspects of the Spanish language is the frequent absence of a written subject. In all different tenses, you will come across sentences where the subject is hidden in the verb conjugation. Focusing on this aspect, and trying to become accustomed to it, is essential in order to achieve the level of command you are looking for. Another important aspect of the Spanish language is that sentences tend to be longer and more complex. Some literary works are actually based on the length of a sentence and one published book has a sentence that goes on for twenty pages, relying only on relative clauses!

However, at this level we will only focus on simple sentences, so there is no need to feel overwhelmed. To achieve a higher level of fluency and comfort, I suggest reading articles and magazines in Spanish, beginning with articles of no more than 20 lines.

We have previously discussed sentence structure, but here is a reminder of the formula you can use to build sentences in the affirmative, negative, and interrogative.

Affirmative Statements

You need at least two elements to form a sentence in the affirmative: **a subject** (a person, an animal, an event, or a thing), **a conjugated verb**, and sometimes you will also need an **object or a complement** that completes the meaning. Here are some examples:

Ella cocina muy bien = She cooks very nicely

La fiesta es en mi casa = The party is at my place

In the above examples, you have a subject (ella, la fiesta), a conjugated verb (cocina, es), and a complement that adds more information to the verbs (muy bien, en mi casa). Remember that in Spanish, the subject can be left out, in which case the sentences would look like this:

Cocina muy bien

Es en mi casa

Remember that you can infer the subject by looking at the ending of the verb.

Negative Statements

As you already know, to form negative statements, you need only to add a negative word, such as no, nunca, or jamás, to a sentence. Here are some examples:

El auto no arranca = The car won't start

Nosotros no comemos carne = We don't eat beef

The negation word goes before the conjugated verb. The structure of a negative statement is quite simple: you need a subject, a negative and conjugated verb. Notice how, unlike English, where you use a bare infinitive after the negative auxiliary, in Spanish, the verb still needs to be in the conjugated form. You can also leave the subject out:

No leemos el diario = We don't read the newspaper

No desayuna en la casa = He/She doesn't have breakfast at home

When you choose to leave out the subject, the sentence begins with the negative word.

Questions

There are several ways to formulate questions in Spanish. We previously discussed three most common ways:

Noun + verb + object

¿Helena toma café?

Verb + noun + object

¿Toma Helena café?

Verb + object + noun

¿Toma café Helena?

All three formulas are correct. You can also use question words like we discussed before, placing them at the beginning of a sentence and shifting the position of verb and noun:

¿Donde toma Helena su café? = Where does Helena drink coffee?

¿Cuánto café toma helena? = How much coffee does Helena drink?

As you can see in the above examples, it is important that the verb be placed before the subject, and the complement can be placed either between these two, before the verb, or after the subject.

Adverbs of Time and Time Expressions

Adverbs of time and time expressions are little pieces of information that will tell you when the action is being done. There are adverbs of time and time expressions for all tenses. When you learn them, you can express how often you do something, when was the last time you did something, or when you expect to do something. Here are some words and phrases for the present simple.

Siempre – always

Todos los días – every day

Todas las semanas – every week

Una vez por semana – once a week

Dos veces por semana – twice a week

Cada día – each day

Frecuentemente - regularly

Seguido, a menudo – often

Muy seguido, muy a menudo – very often

Normalmente, Generalmente - usually

A veces – sometimes

Nunca – never

Casi nunca – hardly ever

You may want to start by identifying verbs and sentences in newspapers and articles and I encourage you to use the list of verbs at the end of the book, in the Appendix, to form your own sentences about your routines and activities.

3 Irregular Verbs in The Present Simple Tense
To make things a little more complicated, we have chosen four main verbs that you will want to use, that belong to the category of **irregular verbs**. Irregular verbs are those verbs where the stem is subjected to changes

when conjugated. Sometimes, only the first person singular (Yo = I) changes. See how to conjugate them for each subject pronoun. Can you identify the changes in the stem?

Infinitive: Tener = To have

Yo tengo = I have

Tú tienes = You have

Él tiene = He has

Ella tiene = She has

Nosotros tenemos = We have

Ustedes tienen = You (plural) have

Ellos tienen = They have

Nosotros **tenemos** una casa con piscina = We have a house with a pool

Tú **tienes** clases esta tarde = You have a class this afternoon

Infinitive: Dormir = To sleep

Yo duermo = sleep

Tú duermes = You sleep

Él duerme = He sleeps

Ella duerme = She sleeps

Nosotros dormimos = We sleep

Ustedes duermen = You (plural) sleep

Ellos duermen = They sleep

Mi madre **duerme** en la otra habitación = My mom sleeps in the other bedroom

Nosotros **dormimos** hasta tarde los domingos = We sleep till late on Sundays

Infinitive: Decir = To say

Yo digo = I say

Tú dices = You say

Él dice = He says

Ella dice = She says

Nosotros decimos = We say

Ustedes dicen = You say

Ellos dicen = They say

Ella **dice** mentiras = She tells* lies

(*in this case, the equivalent is "to tell", which is also a synonym)

Nosotros **decimos** que no = We say no

Verb To Be II: Estar

At the beginning of this book, we learned a little about one of the uses of the verb To Be = Ser. Now we will take a look at the other half of this fascinating verb in Spanish. While in English this is one verb that can be used to express essence or condition, Spanish has two different verbs:

To describe essence: Ser = To be

To describe a condition: Estar = To be

Estar is more dynamic than Ser. The verb Estar represents a condition, a non permanent state that can change in the future. On the other hand, Ser represents an essence.

You can use the verb Estar = *To be* to talk about the following:

Location – Temporary state or condition – The weather – To form the present progressive

Here are some examples:

El cielo está nublado = It is cloudy

El gato está en el techo = The cat is on the roof

Ella está enojada = She is upset

The verb Estar = To be, is an **irregular verb**. We will take a closer look at this verb in the next lesson, when we go over the Present Progressive Tense. Here is how to conjugate the irregular verb Estar, according to each subject:

Yo estoy = I am

Tú estás = You are

Él está = He is

Ella está = She is

Nosotros estamos = We are

Ustedes están = You (plural) are

Ellos están = They are

Ellos están en el jardín = They are in the garden

Nosotros estamos nadando = We are swimming

Present Progressive Tense

The Present Progressive Tense is used to describe actions in progress. There are two parts to the Present Progressive, similarly to its counterpart in English, where a verb *To Be* and an –ing verb are required. In Spanish, you will need to use a conjugation of the verb Estar = To be and present participle.

Present participles can be identified by their endings: -ando, -iendo.

Take a look at these examples:

Ella **está** corr**iendo** = She is running

El perro **está** ladr**ando** = The dog is barking

The distinctive feature of the Present Progressive is that you need a **subject**, **a conjugated verb Estar = To be**, and **a Present Participle**. This last element, the Present Participle, does not need to be conjugated for each subject pronoun. However, it will change depending on the type of infinitive: -ar, -er, and –ir verbs.

Present Participle and –ar verbs.

This is fairly simple to remember, for all –ar verbs, you will need to drop the –ar and add **–ando** to form the present participle. Use a subject and the verb Estar to build a sentence:

Nad**ar** = nad**ando**

Lleg**ar** = lleg**ando**

Ayud**ar** = ayud**ando**

Su amiga está llegando = Her friend is coming

No estoy escuchando = I'm not listening

Estamos mirando la television = We are watching TV

Present Participle With –er and –ir verbs.

Similarly, for all verbs ending in –er and –ir, drop the ending and add –iendo. Here are some examples:

Esconder = escond**iendo**

Vender = vend**iendo**

Aprender = aprend**iendo**

Ella **está** aprend**iendo** francés = She is learning French

Estamos escond**iendo** los regalos = We are hiding the presents

Notice that there are four exceptions to this rule. Because of the morphology of these **four verbs**, a slight variation is needed in order to form the Present Participle:

1. Caer – Cayendo

2. Leer – Leyendo

3. Oír – Oyendo

4. Creer - Creyendo

You will need to **memorize** these, as there are **only four verbs** in this list.

Knowing how to form the Present Participle will help you learn this tense much more quickly. Now it's time to review how to make affirmative, negative, and interrogative statements.

Affirmative Statements in the Present Progressive
You need **at least three elements** to form the Present Progressive in the affirmative: **a subject** (may be hidden in the verb), a **conjugated verb Estar**, and **a Present Participle**. Take a look at these examples:

Su madre **está** cocin**ando** = His mom is cooking

Están habl**ando** por teléfono = They are talking on the phone

In the Present Progressive, the verb that you will have to conjugate is always the verb **Estar = To be**, and then change the main verb accordingly by adding **–ando / -iendo**.

Negative Statements in the Present Progressive

To form negative sentences you need **four essential elements**: **a subject** (may be hidden in the verb), **a negation word**, **a conjugated verb Estar**, and **a Present Participle**. Here are some examples to clarify this concept:

Su madre no está cocinando = His mom isn't cooking

No están hablando por teléfono = They are not talking on the phone

The negative word will come right before the verb Estar = To be.

Asking Questions in the Present Progressive

Just like we previously learned, there is a certain amount of freedom in the structure of questions in Spanish. Here are some acceptable variations:

¿Está su madre cocinando? = Is his mother cooking?

¿Su madre está cocinando? = Is his mother cooking?

¿Está cocinando su madre? = Is his mother cooking?

One rule does not change: the verb Estar is always placed at some point **before** the Present Participle, but never after it.

Also, remember that it is important to use an opening question mark, as well as a closing one.

Time Expressions and Adverbs of Time

These are some useful time expressions and adverbs of time that you can use in the Present Progressive tense.

Ahora = Now

Ahora mismo = Right now

Actualmente = Currently

En este momento = At this very moment

Hoy = Today

Hoy en día = Nowadays

Estos dias = These days

Esta semana = This week

Past Simple Tense

The Preterite or The Imperfect?

In Spanish, there are **two forms** of **the Past Simple: the Preterite and the Imperfect**. The Preterite describes actions and events in the past with a definite beginning and a definite end that are generally considered as complete. It is quite easy to conjugate regular verbs in the Preterite. Here is a chart with the conjugation for regular –ar verbs:

Infinitive: Saludar = To greet

Yo saludé = I greeted

Tú saludaste = You greeted

Él saludó = He greeted

Ella saludó = She greeted

Nosotros saludamos = We greeted

Ustedes saludaron = You (plural) greeted

Ellos saludaron = They greeted.

For all regular –ar verbs, you will need to drop the –ar ending and add one of the following to the stem, according to the subject: -é, -amos, -ó, -amos, -aron. Please notice that the written accent mark is extremely important. While there are a set of rules for using the written accent mark, we will simply mention that the absence of an accent may change the meaning of the word, the sentence, or even change the tense of the verb. So keep your eyes open!

To put regular –er and –ir verbs into the Preterite, simply drop the ending and add –í, -iste, -ió, -imos, -ieron, according to each subject, like in the following examples:

Infinitive: Aprend**er** = To learn

Yo aprend**í** = I learned

Tú aprend**iste** = You learned

Él aprend**ió** = He learned

Ella aprend**ió** = She learned

Nosotros aprend**imos** = We learned

Ustedes aprend**ieron** = You (plural) learned

Ellos aprend**ieron** = They learned

Infinitive: Descub**rir** = To discover

Yo descubrí

Tú descubr**iste**

Él descubr**ió**

Ella descubr**ió**

Nosotros descubr**imos**

Ustedes descubr**ieron**

Ellos descubr**ieron**

Now that you know how to conjugate regular verbs in the Preterite, let's take a look at when to use this tense in writing and conversation.

When to use the Preterite

As a general rule, we can say that the Preterite is used for actions and events in the past that are seen as **completed**, with a definite beginning and a definite end, which can be expressed in the sentence or inferred. These are some of the most common uses of the Preterite:

Single events in the past with a definite beginning and a definite ending (that may or may not be stated)

Ella compró un libro de recetas ayer = She bought a recipe book yesterday

Nosotros hablamos con Cecilia la semana pasada = We spoke with Cecilia last week

The above examples show individual actions that have a beginning and end, with a definite duration.

A series of actions or events in the past, as in a chain of events, or consecutive actions.

Ella diseñó el vestido, lo hizo y lo vendió = She designed the dress, made it and sold it.

You can use the Preterite to describe repeated actions in the past or events that had a specific duration in the past.

Ella vivió en Paris por nueve años = She lived in Paris for nine years

Ellos presentaron tres premios = They presented three awards

You can use the Preterite to state the beginning or ending of an action or event in the past.

Comenzó a llover a las 11am = It started to rain at 11am

La fiesta terminó después de la medianoche = The party ended after midnight

Adverbs of Time And Time Expressions for the Preterite

This is a list of time expressions that will certainly help you identify when the Preterite needs to be used. They all apply to the past.

Ayer = yesterday

Anteayer = the day before yesterday

la semana pasada = last week

el mes pasado = last month

el lunes pasado = last Monday

el año pasado = last year

el otro día = the other day

entonces = then

hace dos meses = two months ago

hace dos años = two years ago

durante tres días = for three days

esta mañana = this morning

esta tarde = this afternoon

Affirmative, Negative, and Interrogative Statements in the Preterite

In Spanish, you need **at least two elements** to build affirmative statements in the Preterite: **a subject** (that may or may not be hidden in the conjugated verb), and a **conjugated verb**:

Ella visitó a los niños = She visited the children

The order of words in the Preterite dictate that it is **an affirmative statement**, the conjugated verb comes after the subject: **subject + conjugated verb + object/complement**. The object or complement is the part of the sentence that adds more information, and may not always be necessary. Here are two more examples:

Nosotros vivimos allí por cinco años = We lived there for five years

Emilia viajó a Israel en junio = Emilia travelled to Israel in June

Negative Statements

To make a negative statement in the Preterite, simply add the negation word **before** the conjugated verb:

Julio no alquiló un auto = Julio didn't rent a car

No escuchamos lo que él dijo = We didn't hear what he said

The negative word – it can be no, nunca, jamás, etc. – goes **before** the conjugated verb. Unlike English, where there is an auxiliary verb, in Spanish the main verb needs to be conjugated to agree with the subject.

Interrogative Sentences

As you already know, questions can be formulated in different ways and still be correct. These are the three most common ways of writing a question in Spanish, in the Preterite:

¿Trabajaste tú aquí? = Did you work here?

¿Tú trabajaste aquí? = Did you work here?

¿Aquí trabajaste tú? = Did you work here?

However, when there is an introductory question word, you need to invert the order of subject and verb. In other words, the conjugated verb will be placed after the introductory word and before the subject:

¿Donde **fue** la fiesta? = Where was the party?

¿Quién prometió ayudarla? = Who promised to help her?

Now that you have a good knowledge of the Preterite, think about past events and try to identify the main verb, using the list of regular verbs that you can find in the Appendix, in the last pages of this book.

The Future Tense

To complete basic knowledge of the Spanish language, you need to know how to talk about events and plans in the future. This tense is quite easy to learn in terms of conjugation, so let's get right into it.

The Future Simple has **three primary uses**, and surprisingly, not all of them refer to the future! Let's start with a simple one: you can use the future simple to talk about actions and events in the future: for example, something that you want to do tomorrow or something that you have decided to do in the near future. Here are some examples:

Veré a Francisco mañana a la tarde = I will meet with Francisco tomorrow afternoon

Cenaré liviano esta noche = I will have a light dinner tonight

You can also use the Future Simple to make assumptions about the present. Because it is not a fact, and you are not certain about what you are stating, the Future Simple indicates a probability that has yet to be proved. Here are some examples:

Vendrá a cenar..= She might come for dinner (assumption/probability)

Él estará mintiendo = He must be telling a lie (assumption/probability)

It is really important to rely on the context to understand whether you are making a statement about the future or an assumption about the present.

Another use of the future simple is to express a strong command. This is not quite common and is often used in advertising, famous phrases, or as a strict request from somebody in authority. Take a look at these examples:

Serás el mejor = You will be the best (from an advertisement)

Notarás la diferencia = You will sense the difference (again, from an advert)

We are ready now to learn how to conjugate regular verbs in the Future Simple. You will discover that this tense is especially easy to conjugate because most of the rules that apply to the other tenses do not apply here.

In other words, you **DO NOT** need to drop the final two words of the infinitive and you do not need to use different conjugations for verbs ending in either –ar, -er or –ir. You will simply need to add one of the endings that agree with each subject at the end of the infinitive, and the endings do not vary regardless of the verb. Let's see some examples to clarify this concept:

For all regular verbs with –ar, -er, and -ir endings, add the following endings to the infinitive: -é, -ás, -á, -emos, -án. Here is an example:

Infinitive: **Comprar** = To buy

Yo comprar**é** = I will buy

Tú comprar**ás** = You will buy

Él comprar**á** = He will buy

Ella comprar**á** = She will buy

Nosotros comprar**emos** = We will buy

Ustedes comprar**án** = You (plural) will buy

Ellos comprar**án** = They will buy

Infinitive: **Comer** = To eat

Yo comer**é** = I will eat

Tú comer**ás** = You will eat

Él comer**á** = He will eat

E la comer**á** = She will eat

Nosotros comer**emos** = We will eat

Ustedes comer**án** = You (plural) will eat

Ellos comer**án** = They will eat

Infinitive: Asistir = To attend

Yo asistir**é** = I will attend

Tú asistir**ás** = You will attend

Él asistir**á** = He will attend

Ella asistir**á** = She will attend

Nosotros asistir**emos** = We will attend

Ustedes asistir**án** = You (plural) will attend

Ellos asistir**án** = They will atend

If you compare the three options, one for each verb ending –ar, -er, and –ir, you will notice that all have the same morphology: the ending is added at the end of the infinitive. You can repeat this with all regular verbs.

Affirmative, Negative, and Interrogative Statements in the Future Simple

In Spanish, you need **at least two elements** to build affirmative statements in the Future simple: **a subject** (that may or may not be hidden in the conjugated verb), and a **conjugated verb**:

Nosotros iremos a Italia = We will go to Italy

As we have discussed before, the order of words in the **affirmative statements** is as follows: **subject + conjugated verb + object/complement**. Sometimes, the subject may appear hidden in the verb. This is perfectly correct and because of it, sometimes a single word may convey the meaning of a whole sentence:

Iré (or Yo iré) = I will go

Negative Statements

To make a negative statement in the Future Simple, you need to add the negation word **before** the conjugated verb:

Ella no recibirá un premio de literatura = She will not receive a literary award

Federico no viajará a Madrid este año = Federico will not travel to Madrid this year

The negative word goes **before** the conjugated verb. Unlike English, where there is an auxiliary verb, in Spanish the main verb needs to be conjugated to agree with the subject.

Interrogative Sentences

These are the **three** most common ways of writing a question in Spanish, in the future simple:

¿Caminará Elisa hasta el lago? = Will Elisa walk to the lake?

¿Elisa caminará hasta el lago? = Will Elisa walk to the lake?

¿Caminará hasta el lago Elisa? = Will Elisa walk to the lake?

However, as we have already discussed in previous lessons, when there is an introductory question word, you need to invert the order of subject and verb.

¿Cuándo regresará Florencia? = When will Florencia come back?

¿Donde dormirá tu hijo? = Where will your son sleep?

Finally, these time expressions and adverbs of time will help you identify and define the Future Tense:

Después = Later

Luego = Later

Pronto = Soon

Mañana = Tomorrow

Esta noche = Tonight

El próximo sábado = Next Saturday

El próximo mes = Next month

La próxima semana = Next week

El próximo año = Next year

El año que viene = Next year

Appendix

Spanish Regular Verbs

This list includes regular verbs with –ar, -er and –ir endings.

Abandonar /a-ban-doh-´nar/ (to quit)

Abrir /a-´brir/ (to open)

Absorber /ab-sor-´ber/ (to absorb)

Abusar /a-bu-´sar/ (to abuse)

Acabar /a-ka-´bar/ (to finish)

Acampar /a-kam-´par/ (to camp)

Acelerar /a-ce-le-´rar/ (to accelerate)

Aceptar /a-cep-´tar/ (to accept)

Admitir /ad-mi-´tir/ (to admit)

Adorar /a-do-´rar/ (to adore)

Alquilar /al-ki-´lar/ (to rent)

Amar /a-´mar/ (to love)

Andar /an-´dar/ (to walk)

Aprehender /a-pre-en-´der/ (to apprehend)

Aprender /a-pren-´der/ (to learn)

Asistir /a-sis-´tir/ (to attend)

Ayudar /a-yu-´dar/ (to help)

Bailar /bai-´lar/ (to dance)

Bañar /ba-´niar/ (to shower)

Barrer /ba-´rrer/ (to sweep)

Beber /be-´ber/ (to drink)

Besar /be-´sar/ (to kiss)

Buscar /bus-´kar/ (to look for)

Caminar /ka-mi-´nar/ (to walk)

Cantar /kan-´tar/ (to sing)

Cocinar /ko-ci-´nar/ (to cook)

Comer /ko-´mer/ (to eat)

Comprar /kom-´prar/ (to buy)

Comprender /kom-prend-´der/ (to understand)

Conceder /kon-ce-´der/ (to concede)

Contestar /kon-tes-´tar/ (to answer)

Correr /ko-´rrer/ (to run)

Cortar /kor-´tar/ (to cut)

Creer /kre-ér/ (to believe)

Cubrir /ku-´brir/ (to cover)

Deber /de-´ber/ (to owe)

Decidir /de-ci-´dir/ (to decide)

Dejar /de-´jar/ (to allow)

Depender /de-pen-´der/ (to depend)

Desayunar /de-sa-yu-´nar/ (to have breakfast)

Describir /des-kri-´bir/ (to describe)

Desear /de-se-ár/ (to wish)

Discutir /dis-ku-´tir/ (to argue)

Enamorarse /e-na-mo-´rar-se/ (to fall in love)

Enseñar /en-se-niár/ (to teach)

Entrar (en) /en-´trar (en)/ (to enter)

Enviar /en-vi-ár/ (to send)

Enseñar /en-se-´niar/ (to teach)

Entrar /en-´trar/ (to enter, to go in)

Esconder /es-kon-´der/ (to hide)

Escribir /es-kri-´bir/ (to write)

Escuchar /es-ku-´char/ (to listen)

Esperar /es-pe-´rar/ (to wait)

Estudiar /es-tu-´diar/ (to study, to revise)

Exceder /ec-ce-´der/ (to exceed)

Existir /ec-cis-´tir/ (to exist)

Firmar /fir-´mar/ (to sign)

Ganar /ga-´nar/ (to win)

Gastar /gas-´tar/ (to spend)

Hablar /a-´blar/ (to talk)

Lavar /la-´var/ (to wash)

Leer /le-ér/ (to read)

Llegar /lle-´gar/ (to arrive)

Llevar /lle-´var/ (to carry)

Mandar /man-´dar/ (to order)

Meter /me-´ter/ (to put into)

Mirar /mi-´rar/ (to look)

Nadar /na-´dar/ (to swim)

Necesitar /ne-ce-si-´tar/ (to need)

Olvidar /ol-vi-´dar/ (to forget)

Omitir /o-mi-´tir/ (to omit)

Partir /par-´tir/ (to leave)

Permitir /per-mi-´tir/ (to allow)

Poseer /po-se-ér/ (to possess)

Practicar /prac-ti-´kar/ (to practice)

Preguntar /pre-gun-´tar/ (to ask)

Prender /pren-´der/ (to switch on)

Preparar /pre-pa-´rar/ (to prepare)

Proceder /pro-ce-´der/ (to proceed)

Prometer /pro-me-´ter/ (to promise)

Regresar /re-gre-´sar/ (to return)

Reparar /re-pa-´rar/ (to repair)

Romper /rom-´per/ (to break)

Saludar /sa-lu-´dar/ (to greet)

Sorprender /sor-pren-´der/ (to surprise)

Subir /su-´bir/ (to go up)

Sufrir /su-´frir/ (to suffer)

Tejer /te-´jer/ (to knit)

Temer /te-´mer/ (to fear)

Tocar /to-´kar/ (to touch)

Toser /to-´ser/ (to cough)

Trabajar /tra-ba-´jar/ (to work)

Unir /u-´nir/ (to unite)

Usar /u-´sar/ (to use)

Vender /ven-´der/ (to sell)

Viajar /via-´jar/ (to travel)

Visitar /vi-si-´tar/ (to visit)

Votar /vo-´tar/ (to vote)

Measurement Conversion

One thing that can be confusing and frustrating is the different systems of measurements applied in the Anglo-Saxon countries and the Spanish speaking world. Here are some equivalencies to help you breach the distance between the two systems.

1 Lb = 0.45 Kg

1 oz = 0.03 Kg

1 mile = 1.61 Km (Kilometers)

1 ft = 0.3 m (meters)

1 in = 2.54 cm (centimeters)

1 gallon = 3.79 l (liters)

1 oz (liquid) = 0.03 l (liters)

Are You Interested In Learning More Spanish?

If so, there are many great e-books on the Amazon Marketplace that can help. Two of the books that we recommend are found here:

<u>Quick Learn. Teach Me Spanish</u>

by Clarisa Rodriguez

<u>SPANISH. An Easy Way to Learn</u>

by Adalina Fuentes

You can get your copy of these great books for your Kindle Fire HD or other e-reading devices and pursue your dreams of learning a second language today or purchase them as a hardcopy as well.

Printed in Great Britain
by Amazon